CONTENTS

Introduction

In the infamous Metropolitan Detention Center in Brooklyn, Ghislaine Maxwell is under constant camera and live surveillance. Her small cell contains a bunk and a steel lavatory. It has no windows. The drinking water is allegedly brown; the food so harshly microwaved as to be almost inedible. She is – this by now is common knowledge – charged with enticement of minors and sex trafficking, on behalf of Jeffrey Epstein. The victims have been interviewed in documentaries and on the news. Hearing their chilling testimony, it's easy to forget that Maxwell's charges have not yet been tested in court – legally, she is still innocent. Well over 90 per cent (some say 97 per cent) of American trials are settled in plea bargains before going to court. Punitive pretrial detention and the prospect of very long sentences put pressure on suspects to enter pleas, admitting some aspects of a crime while withholding others, and sometimes naming names. Maxwell's potential list of names would be media gold, of course, but it would also be of enormous value to prosecutors and politicians eager to show – against all evidence to the contrary – that everyone is equal before the law.

We commissioned the writer Chris Dennis, who knows the inside of American prisons, to write about Maxwell for this issue of *Granta*. His essay is a thoughtful meditation on incarceration, and on sexual predation. Dennis had had many sexual encounters with adults by the time he ran away from home, aged fourteen. He didn't perceive these encounters as abusive at the time – the insight that true consent is predicated on equality, and that the consent he gave was meaningless, came later. 'I had a boundaryless teenage life,' he writes, 'one where I was sought out by deviant adults who pretended they wanted to care for me, while also assuring me that I was mature, that I was like them, even when I was not.'

Kaitlin Maxwell's autobiographical photoessay 'Soft Pink Light', acquired by our new photography editor Max Ferguson, reveals the intimacy of three generations of women. But there is ambiguity here, too. The images – many of them self-portraits – oscillate

The Folio Society

ANGELA CARTER

NIGHTS AT THE CIRCUS

Introduced by SARAH WATERS

With 9 colour and 13 black & white original
lino-cut collages by Royal Academician
EILEEN COOPER

Exclusively available from
foliosociety.com/circus

GRANTA

12 Addison Avenue, London W11 4QR | email: editorial@granta.com
To subscribe go to granta.com, or call 020 8955 7011 in the United Kingdom,
845-267-3031 (toll-free 866-438-6150) in the United States

ISSUE 156: SUMMER 2021

p.182 extract from '1st Light Poem: for Iris – 10 June 1962' by Jackson Mac Low reproduced by permission from the Estate of Jackson Mac Low and Chax Press; p.184 extract from 'The Still Point' by Kwame Dawes originally published on *Harriet*, the blog for the Poetry Foundation, reproduced by permission of Kwame Dawes; pp.182 and 183 extracts from *Letter from a Place I've Never Been: New and Collected Poems, 1986–2020* by Hilda Raz by permission of the University of Nebraska Press. Copyright 2021 by the Board of Regents of the University of Nebraska. Reproduced by permission of Kwame Dawes.

This selection copyright © 2021 Granta Trust.

Granta, ISSN 173231 (USPS 508), is published four times a year by Granta Trust, 12 Addison Avenue, London W11 4QR, United Kingdom.

The US annual subscription price is $50. Airfreight and mailing in the USA by agent named World Container Inc, 150-15, 183RD Street, Jamaica, NY 11434, USA. Periodicals postage paid at Brooklyn, NY 11256.

US Postmaster: Send address changes to *Granta*, World Container Inc, 150-15, 183RD Street, Jamaica, NY 11434, USA.

Subscription records are maintained at *Granta*, c/o Abacus e-Media, 107-111 Fleet Street London, EC4A 2AB.

Air Business Ltd is acting as our mailing agent.

Granta is printed and bound in Italy by Legoprint. This magazine is printed on paper that fulfils the criteria for 'Paper for permanent document' according to ISO 9706 and the American Library Standard ANSI/NIZO Z39.48-1992 and has been certified by the Forest Stewardship Council (FSC). *Granta* is indexed in the American Humanities Index.

ISBN 978-1-909-889-41-5

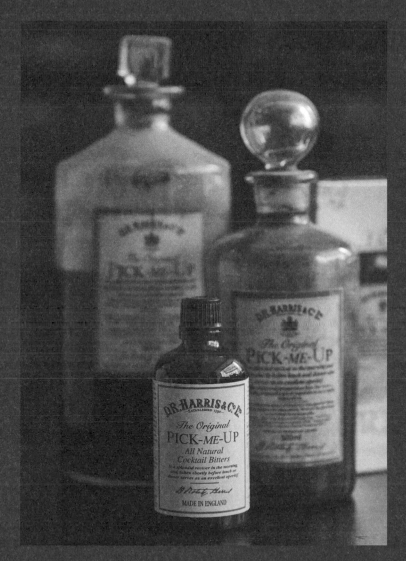

The Original Pick-Me-Up

Introducing the revival of the original morning reviver

29 St. James's Street, London, SW1A 1HD

www.drharris.co.uk | www.originalpickmeup.co.uk

Mslexia Fiction Competition 2021

Your passport to publication

Novel winners and finalists go on to be published at the highest level – visit mslexia.co.uk/submit-your-work/reader-success-stories for recent achievements

Winners and three finalists of both Short Story and Flash Fiction categories will be published in *Mslexia* magazine

24 Short Story and Flash Fiction finalists will be published in the inaugural *Mslexia* anthology *Best Women's Short Fiction 2021*

mslexia.co.uk/competitions
competitions@mslexia.co.uk
(+44) 191 204 8860

NOVEL

For novels of at least 50,000 words by women who are not yet published as novelists

1st Prize: £5,000

JUDGES
HILARY MANTEL
MARIANNE TATEPO
JO UNWIN

SHORT STORY

For complete short fiction up to 3,000 words

1st Prize: £3,000

JUDGE
A L KENNEDY

FLASH FICTION

For complete short fiction up to 300 words

1st Prize: £500

JUDGE
JUDE HIGGINS

mslexia

CLOSING DATE FOR ALL CATEGORIES: 20 SEPTEMBER 2021

between scenes of preparation for exposure to the external gaze and intimate introspection. The scenes are meticulously staged, and so quiet that the implied physical and existential hardship (the lives we imagine beyond the rooms depicted) feels understated, or even concealed. What is at stake here? What is exposed, and what is hidden?

The concept of hardship, or even suffering, is not the only lens through which to see. What Ruchir Joshi calls the image vernacular of Calcutta's misery has been done a thousand times by visiting photographers. His images and text fragments, by contrast, draw attention to unexpected details. The city's infrastructure, one senses, may be breaking under the sheer weight of human footfall, but there are other notes here, too; a mixed track of urban and rural life. Joshi sees, and listens. He is of the city, in the same way that Kaitlin Maxwell is of her family.

Barry Lopez, the acclaimed nature writer, died in December last year. Debra Gwartney, his partner of many years, describes their final weeks together for this issue of *Granta*. It's a heartbreaking story, written with extraordinary precision and restraint. The couple had been made homeless by the violent forest fire that destroyed the part of rural Oregon where they lived – hundreds of houses were evacuated, and many burned to the ground. Lopez's prostate cancer, for a long time kept in check with drugs, turned terminal, and he died in a rented home in the town of Eugene. Gwartney doesn't say so, but Barry Lopez's last essay, the unfinished piece of writing she mentions in her text, was a *Granta* commission. 'On Location' begins with a journey to an Alaskan Yup'ik community, and ends with a chance encounter in the Mojave Desert, where Lopez runs into a man verifying maps and satellite images – a practice called 'ground truthing'. Throughout the text there are references to location; to finding out about place and to finding one's place; to refugees, to destruction, to menacing development. Knowing what we now know, the last line is particularly poignant: 'Today, it's as if every safe place has melted into the sameness of water, and that we're searching for the boats we forgot to build.' ∎

Sigrid Rausing

A SERIES OF
ROOMS OCCUPIED BY
GHISLAINE MAXWELL

Chris Dennis

The Metropolitan Detention Center in Brooklyn is a twelve-storied concrete fortress on the waterfront of New York harbor. When water traffic is low, humpback whales swim through the harbor, feeding on schools of small, silvery menhaden. It's a couple miles from the water's edge to Ellis Island. The detention center possesses the cruel uniformity of a 1950s wedding cake, and houses over a thousand inmates on any given day, almost all of them awaiting trial for federal indictments. It is one of the largest federal detention centers in the United States, but lacks proper heating during the coldest months in the city, and is without adequate air conditioning in the summer. In an enormous system of dysfunctional federal facilities it is the largest and most dysfunctional. There are allegations of rape, racism, sexual misconduct, unsanitary conditions, abuse. People travel from all over the world to visit husbands, brothers and wives who are held here for months and years before they've ever been convicted of a crime. While the building has an industrial, impersonal shape, its very purpose, to imprison human beings, means that it still looks different from the other buildings around it – like an unimaginative concrete leviathan.

Ghislaine Maxwell's cell is small, ten feet by twelve feet. I have been in cells like this. It is like living in a closet, except you are often sharing that closet with two or four other inmates. Maxwell is alone in

9

her cell. She is under constant closed-circuit surveillance. The guards come to check on her every fifteen minutes. This is uncommon. But then it is uncommon for a millionaire to be in a detention center. The historical, horrific truth of the carceral state is that our prisons are filled with poor people. Maxwell is a privileged person in an unprivileged place. Rarer still is that she is a female charged with a sex crime. Nearly all known sex offenders are male. In the detention center where I was held, all of the inmates charged with sex crimes were kept together. You can see the nightmare of this and at the same time understand why it might be necessary. They mostly kept me with other addicts. Jails are segregated, grouping people together by charges, by gender, by race. Women make up only about 4–5 percent of sex crime convictions, and even then, a third of them are convicted alongside a male perpetrator. This doesn't mean that women don't commit sex crimes, but it does mean that women are rarely charged. The majority of the time female perpetrators are poor and uneducated, like most people who are convicted of crimes. A wealthy woman charged with a sex crime seems like an anomaly. Maybe this is part of the reason why, in a world filled with sexual predators, Maxwell's case has gained such enormous attention. And then of course there are the men, the princes and presidents closely linked to her case, who have made the story so sensational. Punishing Maxwell might be a way for us to punish all of the men involved, too – men who might go entirely unpunished. And punishment is the thing that we – our culture, our judicial system – has decided on as the primary solution to crime. As decades of American history continue to accumulate, the crime rates decrease and yet our prisons multiply, filled to capacity in nearly every state.

The language in a federal indictment has a way of wringing the emotion out of a crime, but also revealing how delicately our judicial system is put together, how complicated the burden of proof can sometimes be.

From at least in or about 1994, up to and including in or about 2004, in the Southern District of New York and elsewhere, GHISLAINE MAXWELL, the defendant, Jeffrey Epstein, and others known and unknown, willfully and knowingly did combine, conspire, confederate, and agree together and with each other to commit an offense against the United States, to wit, transportation of minors, in violation of Title 18, United States Code, Section 2423(a).

Even though there are allegedly hundreds of victims, the indictment against Maxwell lists only four. She is accused of enticing each of these minor girls to engage in illegal sex acts. She is accused of grooming them, of using her influence as an older female figure to prime the girls for abuse. These four, all adults now, are the only ones the government has enough evidence to prosecute her for. Maxwell is also charged with perjury, during sworn testimony, about her interactions with the victims. The final charge, appended months after she was arrested, is sex trafficking. That now-so-common and chilling phrase has come to signify a vast underground system of conspiratorial abuse. In Maxwell's case it primarily means that she stands accused of enticing the girls to travel to have sex with Jeffrey Epstein at his Upper East Side Beaux Arts townhouse, his 10,000-acre ranch in Stanley, New Mexico, his private Caribbean island villa, his house on El Brillo Way in Palm Beach and his apartment on Avenue Foch in Paris.

Maxwell grew up the youngest of nine siblings at Headington Hill Hall outside Oxford, a nearly 200-year-old mansion that also housed offices for the publishing company her father owned and operated. Robert Maxwell's work and family life were precisely this inseparable. The mansion is a columned, architectural remnant of nineteenth-century Italian design, splattered with many windows and oak and marble – things you might expect from an English manor. It has fifty-three rooms. It's a place that seems to encourage formality. Robert's widow, Elisabeth Maxwell, writes in her autobiography, *A Mind of My Own*, that her and her children's lives were in service to her husband's needs, to his power and his media empire. He was a millionaire media mogul, originally of Czech Jewish origin, who'd fled the Holocaust (most of his family were killed) to become what some later described as an egocentric sadist. He was notorious for humiliating his employees, while at the same time defrauding millions of pounds from their pension funds. '[Robert] believed duty to him was more important than other demands from the family, that duty came before love,' his daughter-in-law Pandora Maxwell once said. He prized obedience over human connection.

Virginia Roberts Giuffre, one of Ghislaine's most outspoken accusers, first met her at Mar-a-Lago in Palm Beach, Florida, when Giuffre was sixteen years old. Before spending several years in various Florida foster homes, she was a runaway, and had already lived with Ron Eppinger, a 65-year-old sex offender and sex trafficker. Giuffre had just moved back in with her father, and they were both working at Mar-a-Lago. There is a kind of girl Maxwell looked for: vulnerable, unmoored, already sexualized. I was this kind of teenager. My parents, who had been together since they themselves were teens, separated when I was eleven years old. The sudden dissolution of the marriage launched them into a kind of flailing singledom, filled with the agonizing myopia of the poor and newly divorced. Being a gay child in the middle of nowhere, I turned in so many directions for approval. I had already been in multiple sexual relationships with adults by the time I ran away from home at fourteen. I longed for the attention of older men and women and saw my own sexualization by strange adults as a kind of love – a titillating, juvenile version of intimacy. I had a boundaryless teenage life, one where I was sought out by deviant adults who pretended they wanted to care for me, while also assuring me that I was mature, that I was like them, even when I was not. This lie about maturity is something young people crave, that place between autonomy and validation. I wanted to be looked after, and yet also to be told I had power over my own body – a power I often lacked the development to consent to.

The age of consent is a fairly new concept in our culture. Into the early 1900s in the United States, it was between ten and thirteen years old. Delaware law said that a seven-year-old could give consent. It wasn't until later in the twentieth century that states began to push the age restriction to sixteen, then eighteen. One can track the growing evolution of consent laws alongside child development theories. Childhood as an occasion, and children as a protected class, are recent discoveries. As modern psychology transformed the public understanding of children's inner lives, we began to care for them in better ways. Only relatively recently have we started to value a child's humanity over their usefulness, establishing child labor laws as commonplace. The United Nations didn't adopt the Convention on the Rights of the Child until 1989. We have arrived at this moment of global awareness around child sex trafficking not because there's a sudden escalation of powerful men preying on young people, but because we have found a way to name something that's been happening forever.

If the allegations are true, Jeffrey Epstein and Ghislaine Maxwell both exploited the awkward territory of adolescence, to victimize young girls who they knew were already a kind of victim. Perhaps they pretended that they were helping girls like this, giving them money, buying them clothes, taking them on trips, occasionally giving them a place to stay. As if meeting some of the girls' primary needs entitled them to their bodies; as if providing for them gave them a right to abuse them. Perhaps Maxwell and Epstein wanted to live in a more lawless age of entitlement, evidenced most of all by Epstein's unimaginable fantasy to populate his secluded New Mexico ranch with underage girls with whom he would conceive a colony of offspring. In other words, a self-perpetuating sex cult.

I know about being locked in a cell twenty-four hours a day for an indefinite period of time. I know about people who confuse morality for the small jolt of power they get when subjugating hundreds of desperate bodies. I know about waiting, and hiding, and what it feels like when the state is marshaling its resources to punish you. But I also know about systems of predation. I grew up in a charismatic Pentecostal church that claimed, above all else, it wanted to protect children from corruption, while at the same time the leaders of that church were abusing them, including members of my own family. There was an entire structure in place to deliver children to the pastor of our church for sexual abuse, and other systems in place to obfuscate and hide that abuse, much the same way that Epstein and Maxwell are alleged to have built a system to recruit vulnerable, troubled young girls.

But still. If we do not care about what happens to Maxwell, whom do we care about in the criminal justice system? Which criminals do we care about? If the government is going to exercise power over the bodies of its citizens, is it obliged to treat those bodies with dignity? What does it do to the people who work in these institutions, the people who run them, when they do not have to treat prisoners with decency? The prison system is an unending industrial machine. In my home state of Illinois there are twenty-eight operational correctional centers, employing more than 12,000 people. The annual budget for the Illinois Department of Corrections is 1.5 billion dollars. Capitalism, in this way, seems to inevitably lead to the commodification of people, especially vulnerable people.

From 1924 to 1950 Georgia Tann popularized the idea of adoption in the United States by taking children from poor single mothers and selling those children to the very rich. She sold children to Joan Crawford, Dick Powell and the then-governor of New York, Herbert Lehman. She profited from the sale of hundreds of children, and shaped an entire industry around it, laying the foundation for the system of adoption as we know it today. The families of the people she coerced and stole children from had little resources to fight back, but she was also able to continue the practice because she was operating with the notion, widespread in that era, that parents who lived in poverty weren't as capable as parents who had money. She advertised the children as blank slates, tiny people who could be shaped into whatever ideal their new, affluent parents could imagine for them, because wealth made people better. She sold socialites on the idea of better welfare through wealth.

The blinding-white, multilevel superyacht Ghislaine Maxwell's father was sailing when he died is 180 feet long, larger than any house I have ever lived in. The yacht was designed in 1986 by Jon Bannenberg, with a bright, sleek, symmetrical interior, and a flared bow whose bowsprit is like a giant needle piercing the air above the water. I have never been on a boat like this. The yacht is both open and private. A person must feel an immense kind of privacy at sea, out there alone on the water with no sign of the inhabited world. What must it have felt like to be a woman aboard a powerful ship in the 1980s and 90s, before the internet, before location satellites, to have seen the oceans of the world laid out like infinite gardens of glass around you in every direction, as if the water and the sky were the only things that existed other than yourself and the people aboard, most of whom were being paid to serve you? What is the story a yacht tells about what it means to be alive? Robert Maxwell named his yacht *Lady Ghislaine*. She was his youngest daughter. Robert Maxwell died on this boat, or near it, when he disappeared overboard into the Atlantic Ocean in 1991 while sailing off the coast of the Canary Islands. The day after his death the family flew to a nearby airport and made their way to the marina where the yacht was moored. According to one reporter traveling with the family, Ghislaine immediately began shredding documents on board.

On a yacht, you can see anything coming from miles and miles away. Even the laws are different at sea. It is a whole other kind of real estate. I once saw a picture of a prison boat that's anchored off the shore of the East River in New York. It is only ten miles from where Ghislaine Maxwell is now, in her isolation cell at the Metropolitan Detention Center, Brooklyn. The boat is a converted barge, a floating penitentiary that is several stories high and cost 160 million dollars. It's meant to house the overflow from Rikers Island, allowing an increase in the city's inmate population without having to build more prisons on land. No one wants to live next to a prison, so they put them at sea. In the late 1990s the boat was used as a prison for children.

By most reliable accounts, Robert Maxwell introduced Ghislaine to Jeffrey Epstein. Less than a year after her father's death, she had moved in with Epstein and taken on the role of his personal assistant. In the wake of her father's financial crimes, Ghislaine seemed to have offered herself to the service of Epstein, perhaps as a way to maintain the level of wealth that her father had built around her. But also, like her father, Epstein possessed a natural sense of entitlement about the world. Neither of them had come from wealth, and yet they both found a way to amass it in abundance with a kind of cold, sociopathic charisma, and often at the expense of those around them. Her knowledge of their crimes and her apparent willingness to assist them in those crimes bonded her to them. Her value seems defined by them. The inequality of power between the wealthy and the working class, between those who serve and those who are serviced, means that the predatory rich are often in a position to exploit the people around them. Jeffrey might have exploited Ghislaine, but it was an exploitation she would have been familiar with and willing to participate in.

It's hard not to become an abolitionist after spending time in a correctional facility, seeing the marginalized people who end up there, the things that are done to them and the impact they have. But it's the very kind of crime that Maxwell is accused of committing – the routine abuse and exploitation of vulnerable girls – where it becomes most difficult to imagine a society that might collectively advocate for the absolute abolition of prisons. It's the very subject some lawmakers conjure when they want to turn people away from vast criminal justice reform. Sexual crimes evoke a level of community fear and discomfort that denies the nuance we need to transform the role society plays in the creation of crime. But child abuse is a community problem. Sex trafficking is a community problem. We look for someone to blame when it happens, someone to focus all of the attention on, so that we can keep the problem confined. Incarceration is often a way to work around a more complicated issue, but do we want to punish or reform people who commit crimes? Which people do we deem worthy of reform, or capable of it?

I was once a teenager lured into a room by an adult. It is a hard thing to say now. Because at the time I thought, I am a young person having sex with adults because I am special. It is something that I do. It says something good about me that adults consider me a worthy object of desire. It means that I am noticeable. It means that I have power and influence over the world around me. But those are the thoughts of a child. Being an adult now, and a father, I know how very easy it is to not hurt children. As a child I did not know it was easy to not hurt someone. As a child I thought, Oh, it must be very hard for an adult to not have sex with a teenager, because adults are always trying to have sex with me. It was a terrible, uncomfortable room for a young person to be in. I was alone a lot. The word consent meant something very different to me then, because I did not know how to give it.

How does a room make a person who they are. How do the details add up to make a person think and behave a certain way. How does power or money change the way we care for ourselves and for other people? What might being in a prison cell for the rest of her life do to a person like Maxwell. Should we care? What will it make her? Or do we only care about stopping her from being a predator?

There was constant video surveillance in all of the homes where Epstein and Maxwell lived together. When children entered his house, all of their movements and actions were recorded, but also perhaps all of the things that were done to them. Several of Epstein's victims have spoken about the camera systems, and the state purportedly collected some of this as evidence. So how must Ghislaine feel now, being constantly surveilled in a federal jail? Being kept in isolation means to be deprived of regular, natural feedback from the outside world. Is the state just enacting a version of the crime back on the perpetrator, beginning their punishment even before they've ever been convicted? How can we find justice for the victims without becoming culpable in the ongoing injustice of pretrial detention?

The architecture of a prison must age well. It must withstand thousands of people using it every day. Over here we have the permanent iron bench. Over here across from the bed we have the painted concrete wall. The message of the table in a detention center is durability. The message of the open toilet is function over privacy. There is no privacy in state-mandated communal living. Surveillance in a private estate is nearly the reverse of surveillance in a prison, because it inverts the relationship between well-being and power. Denying someone a sense of well-being is a way to have power over them. It seems that Epstein and Maxwell offered girls a version of well-being as an induction, and then renegotiated the terms in order to have control over them. What is the metaphor of the room? Of the house. Of the neighborhood. What does the house say about the neighborhood? What does the house say about the person?

What can the presence of someone like Maxwell teach us about the way we treat people in jails? What can seeing her in this environment, a brutal detention center, show us about the function of the space? There is humanity in thoughtful design, and empathy. Institutions often lack empathy, partly because they are not designed in service of the people who will spend their time there. The public housing project where I grew up has a lot in common with a detention facility. It is an easy transition in some ways from subsidized public housing to incarceration. Those of us who transition from one to the other don't seem out of place there. Jail is a place that is designed to deny people privacy. The space is meant to be convenient for the jailer, and inconvenient for the jailed. What is the difference between the story of a room that is purely functional for many people, versus a room that is decorated and designed for the pleasure of one single individual?

Part of the story of crime and punishment is a story about access to privacy. Poor people are punished more often because they're easier to see and catch. Class, race and education transform the way people interact with law enforcement, and their communities are policed in vastly different ways. Maxwell and Epstein would only have been able to perpetrate the many complicated crimes they are accused of because it took longer for them to be caught. They had so many secluded rooms, which they may have used to commit their crimes in every day for years and years. The exclusive addresses weren't just beautiful real estate, they were secluded, and protected rather than policed. Maxwell and Epstein could flatter and seduce the very people who might charge them with crimes, because they had every opportunity to be alone in rooms with these people, because they were able to buy and create the kinds of rooms that those people would want to spend time in. Maxwell and Epstein used spaces to exert power over children, to manipulate the way they felt and behaved. They used the room to foreshadow what was possible in the room, first saying it would be a kind of massage parlor, by saying the girl in the room was a model. The room was an illusion before it was a crime scene.

It's possible that Epstein was also grooming Maxwell, and that he was preying on her financial circumstances to make her beholden to him, a female adult who could put female teenagers at ease and within his reach. Her presence would have made the girls easier targets for assault, while putting them in situations that made him feel more entitled to their bodies because they had, after all, been paid to touch him. He wanted women in service positions so that he could attempt to expand the boundaries of that service. And Maxwell was another woman in his service.

In a different lifetime, the exact location of their first encounter might have been meaningless, but knowing what we know, it is hard not to give it meaning. The theater of obvious opulence that is Mar-a-Lago makes it easy to imagine someone like Epstein there, and Maxwell, while Giuffre sits in her work uniform – a polo shirt and khaki shorts – reading a book about massage therapy. Maxwell walks up to make small talk, to ask what she's reading, like it's an act of kindness, a guest talking to a staff member. How much money do you give a teenage girl to be alone in a room with a grown man who will inevitably attempt to coerce her into having sex, and not just with him but with his friends, who are also willing to give her money. Mar-a-Lago is a place that desperately wants you to see what it's worth. The story it tells is simply the opposite of poverty. It bears a kind of gold-plated performance of privilege, an ostentatious signal of power and well-being. In this way it's the perfect setting to coerce an at-risk teenager into sex with a grown man. What can the presence of someone like Giuffre teach us about the function of a place like this, about the gap between those who can buy a membership to Mar-a-Lago, and those who work there?

One of the most unsettling, detrimental aspects of being a young person in an intimate relationship with an adult was, for me, trying to navigate the overwhelming, stressful landscape of adult emotions. I was no match for them. I was a child, feeling the things a child feels. I was never going to be their equal, and they knew that, selected me for that very reason, because they wanted to have sex with someone who had less power than them, a teenager who looked up to them, who needed them, who would be under the influence of their experiences and inherent authority. It's this imbalance of authority that makes it abuse. The same inequality of power that makes sex trafficking possible, that makes Maxwell's alleged crimes possible, that makes incarceration possible. This is not so different from the philosophy of the institutionalized body that shapes the carceral state, that allows the prison system to exist at all, that allows the government to use its vast resources to commandeer our rights by criminalizing our suffering – our addictions, our poverty, our mental illnesses. ■

You won't want to miss a word.

Brexit Demise of Great Britain
Rulers of One of the World's Great Powers Go Haywire
Ernie Hasler

Brexit Demise of Great Britain is a political novel that explores many fascinating truths and facts suppressed and falsified by church and state.

£15.95 paperback
978-1-7283-8055-1
also available in ebook
www.authorhouse.co.uk

The Keeper of Families
Jean Heringman Willacy's Afghan Diaries
Sue Heringman

The true story from diaries and audio-tapes of an intrepid American woman's adventurous life in Afghanistan and her later tireless efforts helping Afghan refugees rebuild their lives with dignity.

£15.95 paperback
978-1-7283-8064-3
also available in hardcover & ebook
www.authorhouse.co.uk

A Life Above the Line – Just!
C. P. (Charles Pierre) Altmann

This fun fictional biography of Christoph Aitkin, an inveterate gambler, depicts a career in the advertising industry during the late twentieth century, through his own eyes and very human approach.

£13.95 paperback
978-1-7283-5675-4
also available in ebook
www.authorhouse.co.uk

Heirs of Deceits
Elizabeth Reinach

Sir Gilbert was rejected by his social class because he first hired his illegitimate children as servants, then recognised them, to the world's horror. Murder and chaos followed.

£13.99 paperback
978-1-9845-8983-5
also available in hardcover & ebook
www.xlibrispublishing.co.uk

The Cure
Sandra Freeman

Dany returns to France in an effort to heal her heartbreak and discovers an exclusive hotel where love overtakes, consumes, and alters Dany to the depths of her soul.

£10.95 paperback
978-1-7283-5204-6
also available in hardcover & ebook
www.authorhouse.co.uk

Me Jane
Jane Waller

Poignant and personal, this, her nineteenth book, is a memoir of the artist and writer's 1950s UK childhood, and the shifts that altered her and her family forever.

£27.71 paperback
978-1-7283-5228-2
also available in ebook
www.authorhouse.co.uk

Sasha Debevec-McKenney

THE STARS OF THE *FAST & FURIOUS* FRANCHISE HAVE A CLAUSE IN THEIR CONTRACTS THAT SAYS THEY CAN NEVER LOSE A FIGHT

All last fall I shouldn't have been driving.
I knew what a car could mean to a person and what a person
could mean to a person and I drove off the road instead.
I didn't really want to die.
Instead of saying I want to die
we should say I want to go to sleep.
We want pause. We want to hold ourselves in slow motion
having just driven off a cliff, to close our eyes and feel
the parachute pull us back, take a deep breath as the car flies
between two skyscrapers. Another spring, another sequel.
Give me Tyrese and Ludacris burning circles
into the moon, Michelle Rodriguez flipping
in zero gravity, Vin Diesel racing a spaceship to Mars
and winning. The franchise branches out.
The world introduces new villains.
I was not an Angry Drunk but fuck
I am an Angry Sober. Sobriety empties
all the hiding places. The world becomes a straight line.
You look Hate in the face like an old friend.
I never pictured getting the gang back together like this –
bare, alight, clamoring for a seat.
Paranoia keeps checking the airbag.

We pull up on Everyone Is Looking At Me
while he's in a meeting. I tap on the glass door and motion,
come with me. There is mounting sexual tension.
Disordered Eating has to tuck her daughter in for a nap.
She'll meet us at HQ, wearing something much tighter.
A Consuming Fear Of Death is out back in the garden.
He thought he had retired from this life.
I shake my head and he throws down his shovel.

AMBER BAVERSTOCK

IN THE AFTERMATH

Eva Freeman

The night we moved Uncle Raleigh's cold body into the dining room, the only one in the apartment with a working air-conditioning unit, his spirit rose up again and teetered the few steps to our bedroom door, wheezing all the way. I slept right through the resurrection but woke to Isaiah, my five-year-old brother, trembling on the floor beside my bed, tangled in his sweaty pajamas.

'He won't leave me alone,' he moaned, shoving his thumb into his mouth.

His bladder had released itself in fright. I could smell it on him even before I slid to the floor and touched his damp pajama pants. It was a warm, yeasty smell like freshly baked bread. In the partial light of the street lamp, Isaiah's face glistened with snot and tears.

I picked him up and changed him into fresh pajamas, all the while cursing Uncle Raleigh's selfishness. Isaiah had always been his favorite. But we needed to sleep, especially Mama, who was working an early-morning shift at the rehab center. I left Isaiah curled in the safety of my comforter and went to test the dining-room door. The brass ring around the knob was loose, but the lock held. I leaned my ear against its plywood surface. Nothing moved behind it. Nothing alive at least, I thought. When I returned I locked our bedroom door, and for good measure placed a chair under the knob.

A few hours later, I found Mama in the kitchen hunched over a cup of coffee at our small breakfast table. We lived on the third floor, the top floor, and the morning sunlight poured in through the room's only window. A thin film of dust and cobwebs covered the pane, but still the light was beautiful.

'Isaiah can't sleep,' I said. 'He thinks Uncle Raleigh is after him.'

She turned her face away from me and wiped her eyes with the corner of her scrubs. Mama always seemed better than her surroundings and nothing made that more clear than when she was dressed in her scrubs, freshly showered. The burgundy V-neck exposed a patch of well-oiled skin warm with the scent of shea butter. And around her neck hung three gold chains, one with a cross, another with a diamond chip and the last sporting two discs with our first initials in the center of them: 'I' and 'R'. Isaiah and Remi. 'I' and 'R' always above her heart, on her breastbone day in and day out, against the rhythm of her heart. She straightened but, still keeping her back to me, took her coffee cup to the sink. That effort alone seemed to cow her, and she paused over the aluminum basin, both hands braced against its edge.

'I called and the earliest they can take him is tomorrow,' she said.

Two weeks before, the rehab center where Mama worked on Caton Avenue erected a white tent behind the hedges that lined its circular drive. Unlike the other centers, they hadn't been hit very hard, but one day she came home exhausted from work and took to bed for a week. We tried our best to avoid her. We wore masks inside and washed our hands, rubbing the soap between our fingers, scrubbing our thumbs, encircling our wrists then the fingertips and the nails just like she'd taught us. But when she started feeling better, Uncle Raleigh started coughing. He'd washed his hands but refused to wear a mask. It didn't seem to register with him that there was something lurking, unseen and dangerous, in the air. At seventy-five years old, he didn't believe in anything that he hadn't already witnessed with his own two eyes. So when he came down with chills and a cough, none of us were surprised. I could see the fear in him. For once he didn't fight with Mama about going to see a doctor. He spent an hour in the ER and then they sent him home. Hundreds were either sick or dying. They had white trailers, Uncle Raleigh reported, set up in the hospital's parking lot to house the dead.

Isaiah was still sleeping when Mama left. I checked the dining-room door again. I pressed my ear against the plywood. I could hear a slight hitch in the air conditioner's grinding tone, nothing more.

I returned to the kitchen and pulled the iPad from its place on the shelf above the counter. It was sleek and smooth beneath my fingers. I moved into the narrowing patch of sunlight at the breakfast table and swiped upwards on the screen. The Department of Education had sent an iPad to every student who needed one. I was already familiar with the technology because of my Saturday enrichment course at Medgar Evers College. Ms Melendez, my art teacher, had recommended me for it after our class on Gauguin.

'What do you see?' she asked us. On the SMART board was an image of a young brown girl lying naked on a bed. Her ankles were crossed, and her arms were set akimbo. Her face was turned toward us, the viewers, with a few strands of dark hair covering her cheek. She looked about fourteen years old and easily could have been one of the students in our class.

'I see her ass,' Matthew said, and the boys sniggered.

Ms Melendez's dusky skin flushed hot pink. She was new to PS 425, the third art teacher we'd had in three years. They didn't last long in a room set up with communal tables and free access to scissors, paper and glue. There were thirty of us in all, and it was impossible for a teacher at the front of the room to keep an eye on each and every one of us. I could see Ms Melendez second-guessing her decision to show this slide to a bunch of eighth-graders and, for some reason, I felt a pang of sympathy for her. I raised my hand.

'Yes,' she said. 'I'm sorry. What is your name again?'

'Remi,' I said.

'Remi,' she said. 'Yes, of course, Remi. Tell me, what do you see?'

'Besides her ass,' Matthew shouted again.

'She's too young,' I said, ignoring him.

'What do you mean, she's too young?' Ms Melendez asked.

'I see a teenager who has been told what to do, how to lie there on the bed. She doesn't look comfortable. She looks like she is trying to make herself comfortable. But you can tell. It's like some weight is pressing down on her. Maybe it's the weight of all of us looking at her.'

Ms Melendez turned to the painting and then stepped backward to squint at it. In a quiet voice she said, 'Yes, yes, I see what you mean.'

A week later, during parent–teacher conferences, she handed Uncle Raleigh a brochure for Ifetayo. He would have forgotten about it if I hadn't reminded him later that evening when Mama got home. He pulled it out of his pocket and handed it to her. She looked at it and said, 'Your art teacher gave you this? Not your English teacher or your math teacher?' I nodded. 'That school,' she murmured. But the next week, she signed me up for the program. There were ten of us in all. We met in the English Department's computer lab. Every week there was a different guest lecturer who taught us about 'the value, strength and creativity of the African diaspora', and then we were allowed to use the computers to explore whatever topic or idea that appealed to us.

After an hour of virtual school, I took a break and went to the bathroom, where I found Isaiah crouched in the small space between the toilet and the bathtub.

'I can hear him,' he moaned. I picked him up and held him against me on the toilet seat.

'You can't hear him,' I reasoned with Isaiah. 'He's in the dining room and he's being really, really quiet.'

He reared back in my arms. His eyes were the size of saucers, the whites rolling in panic. He was crying so hard he was hiccuping, rocking back and forth in my lap. Mama told me once that rocking back and forth was something that her mentally disturbed patients did to soothe themselves. I picked him up and carried him down the hall to Andrea's room.

We shared the floor with her. It was essentially a railroad apartment with the kitchen in the back. The three bedrooms, dining room and living room alternated on either side of the central hallway. Technically, it was an illegal sublet, but we needed the extra cash and Andrea was family. Mr Pinckney owned the entire building and lived on the first floor. In the three years we'd lived there, I'd never seen him in anything but a wife beater, boxer shorts and flip-flops. Nothing in his life seemed to require him to dress properly. If anything in our apartment broke, he called an old Jamaican man with salt-and-pepper locs that reached down his back. He'd trudge up the dark stairway with his aluminum box of tools and sigh at the groaning plumbing. His fixes only lasted a month or two and then Mama was back downstairs yelling at Pinckney.

I knocked on Andrea's door.

'What?' she snapped. She opened it just wide enough to stick her face out. Her room in normal circumstances would have been the living room, and she'd covered its three front windows overlooking 21st Street with floral-patterned bed sheets. She couldn't afford blinds or regular curtains because she'd blown all her money when she first arrived in the city on a fifty-five-inch flat screen. It hung over the bureau on the opposite side of the room and played music videos all day and all night.

'I need you to watch Isaiah,' I said, shifting him from one hip to the other.

'I've got a customer,' she said, glancing over her shoulder.

I leaned forward to catch a glimpse of a middle-aged Black woman in a chair at the end of the bed. Her head was covered in half-inch starter locs that were matted together into one tangled mess. She wore a mask, but I could tell from her eyes that she was smiling weakly behind it, as though embarrassed by her own vanity. I turned back to Andrea. She wasn't wearing a mask. Mama didn't want her doing hair in the apartment, but just like the rest of us, Andrea had to make rent.

'He's scared of Uncle Raleigh,' I said, lowering my voice. 'Just let him sit in the back and play on his games. He won't bug you.'

'For how long?' she asked.

I glanced at Isaiah and back at her.

'A half an hour,' I said. 'Tops,' I added when she frowned at me. 'I've got to get something that will make him less scared.'

'We're all scared,' she said. 'This country needs prayers.'

A month ago, at the start of the pandemic, someone tagged the USPS mailbox on the corner. The neon-blue bubble letters were supposed to spell out initials but in their current state looked like a single, abstract shape, outlined in fire-engine red. It glowed like something out of a museum, still communicating the energy and movement of its making. The term came to me when I turned the corner onto Flatbush: 'abstract expressionism'. I stood under the red awning of Crisp and Crunchy Kennedy Fried Chicken waiting for the traffic light to change. On a normal day, Flatbush moved. Cars leaped forward at intersections, darting ahead to be the first to turn. Delivery trucks, ignoring oncoming traffic, parked in the middle of the road and diverted the steady stream of steel and chrome into improvised channels. Drivers climbed down from their perches, walked around back and lifted the doors with a great clattering of steel. They pulled long ramps from inside, setting off choruses of clanks and clatters, delivering cans of beer, ice cream and sodas – whatever the surrounding stores needed. But that day on the street corner at the height of the pandemic there was only one sound dominating the heavens, the long continuous wail of emergency vehicles. Just when one siren completed its circuit, another took up the call.

I crossed the street, headed toward the deli with the sun-bleached ads, featuring benefits-approved products. They were faded into pastel colors that I associated, for some reason, with California sunshine: Kool Aid, Trail Mix Crunch, Special K, Multigrain Krispies, Hunt's Ketchup and something called Tang Orange. There was another tag by the mailbox artist, only this one with black bubble letters outlined in red. It marked the side of a shoe store. In the crevices and corners of door frames and gates were business cards for Poblanita Car Service and blue-and-white stickers for Frankie's

Locksmith and Hardware. Commerce here was reduced to its barest form, the slogan, and was only interrupted by the presence of Jesus in all his incarnations: Eglise De Dieu De Beree. Church of God Faith in Christ. Church of the Holy Innocents. Rescue the Perishing Deliverance Ministries Intl. Inc. Upon this Rock Church of God. Triumphant Church of God.

After this, the heat and slogans of Flatbush gave way to massive brick apartment buildings that spanned entire blocks. Sicko and CSR-1 had tagged the first-floor walls of each. Otherwise there was little to distinguish one complex from the next. They felt otherworldly, even a little sinister, in their total devotion to housing as many people as possible. At least here it was always quiet.

On Ditmas Avenue, trees lined the lane. Twenty in all reached sixty feet into the air and, with their sweeping branches, weaved a canopy of leaf stippled green across the heavens. The air here was moist and cool from their recycled breath. Birds nested in the soft-barked trunks and their offspring chattered and circled in the highest branches like singing garlands. Above, the sheltering emerald green was interrupted by fragments of white and the sky's Berlin blue like shattered pieces of Chinese porcelain.

The homes here spread around corners, and the sirens, largely concerned with the other side of Ocean Avenue, faded into a manageable wail. Wide front porches invited rest. There were cupolas and rotundas, towers and verandas. The lawns out front were of equal importance. Already tulips had opened and sagged under the weight of their own meaty petals, exposing two or three thready pistils at their centers. Hedges and ferns grew in pleasing, alternating patterns of meticulous shades of greenish blue, greenish white and greenish black. Wide windows opened onto empty passageways of varnished wood that hinted at unencumbered movement, and what I imagined was unencumbered thought. Most were empty, their owners having fled at the start of the pandemic to their vacation homes outside of the city.

At the end of March, right before he got sick, turning onto 18th, Uncle Raleigh and I heard something moving at great speed, and then trying with great effort to slow itself. That sound in and of itself wasn't unusual, but what followed stopped us dead in our tracks. It was the showering down of a thousand tiny pieces, as something that was once solid and complicated came apart, splintering into ever smaller bits of plastic and steel. By the time we arrived at the corner a young Black man was pacing back and forth in the intersection, his arms rising and falling to the rhythm of his agitation.

'Oh my God. Oh my God,' he said. 'He ran the stop sign. He *ran* the stop sign. Why didn't he stop at the stop sign?' A young teenage girl dressed head to toe in black with thick braids cascading down her back stood silently amid the destruction. She held a plastic soda bottle in her hand. Her stillness suggested she had been the passenger in the young man's car. It was a cheap Japanese model, built low to the ground for stealth and speed. The impact had spun it around so that it faced back the way it had come. The front half was ripped open. A piece of Styrofoam shaped just like the front fender lay in the street, although its black casing was nowhere to be found. The car's intestines, wires and jagged pieces of white plastic, spilled onto the concrete below.

Uncle Raleigh whistled when he spotted the other vehicle. It was a minivan. The impact had catapulted it over the corner, so that it rested perpendicular to the sports car, wedged on top of a hedge and the adjacent apartment building's low brick wall. We crossed the street for a better view and found the van's entire right side caved in. The passenger-side door was open and a deployed airbag covered its side window. Leaning against the car cushion, propped half in and half outside of the van, with her feet braced against the cement, was a middle-aged white woman. She pressed a cell phone to her ear.

'I don't know,' she moaned into it. 'I don't know what happened.' Her right knee looked just a little bit off. 'All I know is that I need help,' she screamed into the phone.

The driver, an elderly man, hunched over at the waist, unable to straighten his spine, hobbled around the front of the van to her side. His short-sleeved button-down shirt swung open with his efforts, revealing a white undershirt. He wore black dress socks pulled up high over his calves and a pair of shorts that stopped at his knees. He didn't say anything but hovered around the damaged door. The woman refused to make eye contact with him, and when I glanced down at her knee again, it was fatter and turning a deepening shade of purple.

'He ran the stop sign,' the young man yelled to no one in particular.

An audience had gathered on each of the intersection's four corners. Most looked like residents from the surrounding apartment buildings, clots of older women, drawn from their early dinner cooking into the street. On this one stretch of Newkirk, there were no Victorian homes. A middle-aged woman came to stand beside us. She wore a thick nylon shower cap. Her stomach escaped the gap between a tank top and the Lycra binding of her bicycle shorts. It was loose and flabby like the spilled pancake batter that sometimes escaped the lip of our mixing bowls.

Uncle Raleigh glanced away when he saw her. His grip tightened on my hand. I looked down at his knuckles. Between those carved mahogany knobs the valleys where the lotion could not reach were light with ash. In Bahia, one of the Brazilian outposts of the African diaspora I'd learned about at Ifetayo, Uncle Raleigh would have been considered 'root', as grizzled and gnarled as the thick ropes growing from the base of a baobab tree. 'Root' meant you were closer than others to Africa in thought, language and dress. One such tree was estimated to be over two thousand years old, and even though Uncle Raleigh was a second-generation American, he possessed that same quality of endlessness. He stood up straighter in this woman's presence, as though his spine were the mast to a ship that could rescue us all from colonialism's indignities – like Lycra, and nylon and the processed foods that reduced this queen's stomach to a spreading, sagging rumble.

I had also seen and felt that stinging lash of his disdain. Uncle Raleigh coddled Isaiah with a tenderness that he could never muster for my mother and me. Bouncing Isaiah on his knees, delighting in the toddler's drooling glee, Uncle Raleigh would send me running to fetch things for him, claiming, if I hesitated for even a moment, that I 'had young legs and should use them'. I always felt like a broom's handle beneath his ashy grip. He had never married. A fact that my mother rarely if ever mentioned because of what it might mean. But whatever shame had shackled him radiated from his entire being, turning him into an unforgiving judge, critical of the slightest human defect.

Granted, when my father dragged me to a paternity test to establish that I was truly his, Uncle Raleigh intervened. My father had been raised better, Uncle Raleigh said, but we knew that wasn't entirely true. As the youngest, he had been allowed to grow up wild on the streets. 'He always did seek pleasure for pleasure's sake,' my mother explained to me after that tearful visit to the paternity testing center on Church Avenue. The billboard out front had a picture of a fat, white baby and the slogan, DOES HE REALLY HAVE HIS FATHER'S EYES? In the waiting room, I'd looked at my father, a vision of pecan-colored beauty but sweaty now from his effort to prove his delusions true, an excuse to leave us. Even as I gazed at him with the sympathy and pity that only a child can feel for a parent, I knew that he would never test Isaiah in this way. His disappointment in me was an extension of his disappointment in my mother. Uncle Raleigh came to our rescue, moved in with us when my father disappeared, and watched over us, always with that cutting, unrelenting eye. The same one he cast now on that poor woman who had stepped from the privacy of her home onto that most public of street corners.

The adjacent building's super, Mr Watt, an old friend of Uncle Raleigh's, also joined the mayhem in the intersection. He wore his blue work shirt with his name stitched onto the front and his dark blue work pants. His fat key ring slapped with authority against his thigh. He pointed to the heavens, the north, the south, now east, now west, as he reported the accident on his own cell phone, no doubt to the building's management company.

'Watt,' Uncle Raleigh called out. 'You see what happened?'

Watt crossed the street without lowering his cell phone. 'You know these young Black men,' he said. 'They make me so angry. They don't always behave the way they should. They have problems.'

'But he says the van ran the stop sign,' I called out.

'No, no,' Watt said, shaking his head. He had a thick French accent, but I never knew where he was from exactly.

'He was going too fast. You see the marks. He tried to stop but he couldn't.'

The young driver was on his phone too. 'I just know these cops,' he moaned. 'You don't know how they are. They'll find a way to pin it on me. They'll find a way to send me back.'

It occurred to me as we walked away to complete our bottle-returning errand on Newkirk that we would never really know what happened at the intersection.

N ow, halfway down the block on Newkirk under the scaffolding that had been there since early February, I found a green glass bottle. It was for an expensive French brand, and I knew that I had made the right decision to cross Ocean Avenue. Green would work but blue, cobalt blue to be precise, would be better. I'd learned that in the Congo people hung shards of broken ceramic plates and cups from the trees. It was believed that the sound they made on the wind, the clinking and clanking of porcelain, drew evil spirits to them. Down South slaves had turned the ceramics into bottle trees. They hung blue- and green-colored glass bottles from the myrtle tree's branches. The colors drew evil spirits to them. Once inside, they couldn't escape the narrowed necks and were burned away by the morning sun. It was old magic, root magic, the only thing that could capture and contain someone like Uncle Raleigh.

I passed the 'Murder Mart' on the corner of 17th and Newkirk. Of course that wasn't its official name. Officially it was the Smoke and Deli shop. Beside their dumpster and recycling, white cathedral candles encircled several blue cathedral candles on the ground. Someone had also splashed blue paint onto the cement around them. The color marked the block as Crips territory, and just as I wondered about their fallen comrade, a police cruiser pulled up alongside the makeshift shrine. I bowed my head and continued down the street past the Mexican tienda, the Haitian church, the fish store and the gyro cafe with its faded sign announcing its grand opening in January still hanging in the display window. I turned the corner at 16th Street. About a quarter of the way down the block were the bottle and can exchange machines. The grocery-store owners had marked the sidewalk at six-feet intervals with long strips of red tape. It occurred to me, as my fellow bottle scavengers avoided eye contact or stepped into the gutter to avoid me, how much the virus had exploited our weakness for connection. It made everyone suspect. I cleared my throat behind my mask.

'Excuse me,' I called to the man six feet in front of me at the end of the line. 'Do you know where I can find blue bottles?'

'No, no, no,' he said, shaking his head for emphasis. I stepped down into the gutter and pulled out my flip phone. It had taken me fifteen minutes to walk from Flatbush to Newkirk. I still had time. A great rattling came from around the corner. A few seconds later, an older gentleman pushing a grocery-market cart appeared from behind it. Broom and mop handles were staked at each corner of its metal frame. From them he'd tied two bags packed full of aluminum cans and plastic bottles. The cart was piled high with stuffed bags and three additional ones hung from its front handle. He shimmered and rattled as he walked, the insides shining iridescent and metallic in the overcast light. He wore a fedora cocked to the side and a button-down shirt that was open at the neck. A jaunty handkerchief was tied around his throat. He looked like someone out of a Van Der Zee photo, transported through time with that same air of dignity that everyone in the sepia-toned portraits seemed to possess.

'Excuse me,' I said, clearing my throat again. 'Excuse me,' I repeated a little louder.

'What can I do for you?' he asked.

'I'm looking for blue bottles, sir,' I said. I wondered at my use of the honorific. I'd never used it on Uncle Raleigh before and he by right would have deserved it more than the scavenger before me.

'Blue bottles?' he asked. I nodded. 'No money in those.'

'I don't need them for the money,' I said. 'I need them for –' I stopped myself. 'An art project,' I finished lamely.

'Your art teacher sent you out in a pandemic to collect bottles?' he asked.

'Well, no,' I said.

'What do you need them for then?'

We imagined he'd died in his sleep. His body was cold when Mama went in to wake him at 5 a.m. before she left for her morning shift. The ambulance took almost an hour to arrive and when she opened the door, there was only one EMT standing in the hallway.

'Don't you work in pairs?' she asked, leading him toward Raleigh's bedroom door.

He mumbled something.

'What?' she demanded. 'Speak up.' I knew that tone. The EMT had no choice but to answer.

'He had an emergency at home,' he said.

She'd spoken to him as though he were a child, and when I saw him I understood why. He looked eighteen years old, if that. His eyes were bleary and red-rimmed. His hair, perhaps hours before, had stood upright in spikes, shaped and formed by hair gel, but at the end of the shift they'd deflated. A thin gold chain hung around his neck.

'Where . . . ?' he asked.

'In the bedroom,' my mother added, leading him toward the back. At the doorway, she turned on me. 'Remi,' she said, 'go make your brother breakfast.'

I lingered, trying to peer around her into the room.

'Now,' she said.

I poured Isaiah a bowl of cereal and settled him into his seat.

I could hear the mattress creaking rhythmically as though someone was pressing hard down on something on top of it. Was he doing chest compressions? I wondered. On a dead body?

'Time,' my mother said.

The door opened and the EMT walked into the hallway. He didn't notice me there. His eyes were made of glass, wide open, the size of saucers but blind. He stumbled toward the front door.

'You can't leave,' my mother called after him, 'until you contact the morgue and they come to pick up the body. You have to wait here with us.'

'Lady,' he said, turning on her with the first sign of gumption he'd displayed since his arrival, 'there's no one to call. There's no more room. Anywhere.'

'I don't understand,' she said.

'We've been on call since 7 p.m. last night. Back-to-back calls all the same. Cardiac arrest. Cardiac arrest. We tried chest compressions for forty minutes. Then they told us just do it for twenty because the calls keep coming. We were on our way home when we got this one. Twenty minutes of chest compressions but –' He turned to her now, his face pleading with her to put an end to this. 'I volunteered for this because I thought it would look good on my résumé. I'm a freshman at CUNY. I wanted to work for one of the big firms, but now they're telling us to keep the bodies in air-conditioned rooms and for you to reach out to local funeral homes.'

My mother just stared at him.

What did I need the bottles for? This stranger wanted to know. I needed the bottles because there was a dead body in our dining room. Because it was still chilly out but we had to keep the air conditioner on to slow its decomposition. Because my mother had to work. Because my father had left. And even though I didn't believe in ghosts, I could feel him in that room just behind that flimsy door, waiting for us to join him.

'I need the bottles because my dead uncle is haunting my brother, Isaiah, and he's too scared to sleep. And he needs to sleep because he's little. He's haunting Isaiah because Isaiah was his favorite, not me because I'm just a girl. There's no room at the morgue or the funeral home, so we put his body in the dining room with the A/C –'

'The body is in the dining room?' The scavenger interrupted me. He no longer wore his jolly grin. It was as though he had been told something that he'd suspected all along, horror blossoming within him like nightshade.

'We need the blue bottles to capture his spirit so that the morning sunlight can burn it up and send him to the trees on Ditmas Avenue.'

'Jesus, Mary and Joseph,' he said. He wiped his hand over his face.

'Don't touch your face,' I wanted to yell at him.

'Saratoga water,' he said. 'That used to come in blue bottles.'

He continued to shake his head, mumbling something to himself as he arranged and rearranged the bags in his cart. It was as though the story about Raleigh had knocked something loose in his mind, and the professional demeanor that had first impressed me was replaced by the image of a confused and doddering old man.

I knew of three places on Newkirk that might sell that kind of water. All three during better times had outdoor seating. We passed them on our way to the playground at PS 135 on the corner of Coney Island Avenue. The customers looked like people out of advertisements. Even on the darkest, gloomiest, most overcast days, they looked well lit. They seemed to know that they were on display but, sipping coffees or crumbling croissants through their fingertips, they didn't seem to care what the onlooker thought of them. Some wore sunglasses. Some worked on sleek laptops, but none of them ever seemed interested in Uncle Raleigh, Isaiah and me. They appeared lost in the pleasure of consumption, the pretty food on their plates that was too beautiful to eat. They must, I thought, half running, half walking, have blue bottles.

The first one was a small French bistro on the corner, only two blocks away. Their outdoor benches were empty, but I went around the side in search of their recycling. There was only one bag, and I tried to see through it. The sidewalk was sticky with garbage and the recycling's residue. Grime and food drippings streaked the green dumpster beside the bag. Every surface was gummy and the faint odor of sour milk wafted from the bag in my hand.

'Can I help you?' a voice asked from behind me. I turned from my scavenging to see a man standing in the side doorway with a white apron wrapped around his waist.

'Can I *help* you?' he asked again.

'I'm sorry,' I stammered. 'I'm just looking for Saratoga water bottles . . . ?'

'Wait here,' he said. He disappeared inside and came back out with two full water bottles.

'You mean something like these?' he asked, holding them up to the light. I felt like I was looking up at the linden trees. The garbage, the tags, the spilled blue paint, the pigeon-streaked awnings, the dust and the dirt disappeared in the light of the blue. They were regal urns, vessels, owned by kings and queens who had them buried along with their bodies when they died. They reminded me of the shards of pottery and glass on display at the Met, beautiful in both their form and function. The blue was almost opaque, impenetrable, certainly strong enough to contain Raleigh's restless spirit.

The stranger handed me the bottles, and I cradled them in my arms.

'I don't have any money,' I said.

'That's okay,' he said. 'Hang on a minute.' He disappeared back inside. Just when I thought he had forgotten about me, he reappeared with a grease-stained brown paper bag.

'Here,' he said, 'put the bottles in here. I also made you a burger. I'm trying out a new recipe while we're closed. So, you'll have to come back sometime and let me know if it was any good.'

'Thank you,' I said. I couldn't say much more. It wasn't the food that silenced me but the fact that he hadn't asked me to explain about Raleigh and the body or Isaiah's fear or my own loneliness. He just anticipated what I needed and, for the first time in a long time, I felt held in generosity's gentle embrace. I turned before the tears leaked out. I got pretty ugly when I cried. My nose turned bright red and my mother could spot it, even when I tried to hide my sorrow from her. She had a nurse's eye for pain, a way of sensing the discomfort of others.

'First,' I said to Isaiah back in the apartment, 'we eat.' I took out the foil-wrapped burger and placed it on a plate. There were fat fries and a dill pickle too. I arranged them the way I had seen them arranged on the plates at the cafes.

I grabbed a serrated knife from the stand on the counter and cut the burger in half. The meat was thick and dense. It was held between an English muffin, and I raised my half doubtfully to my lips. Maybe it had been easy for him to part with the burger because he knew it was an unsuccessful attempt at something different or maybe he just liked poisoning little girls who were found rummaging through his garbage. I took a bite and closed my eyes against the pleasure of it. Relief radiated through every muscle and joint in my body. I hadn't realized I was hungry. I'd skipped breakfast. Isaiah murmured his approval and wiped a rivulet of grease from the corner of his mouth.

'Hang on,' I said, and ripped a paper towel off the roll on the counter. I understood why the people at the cafe felt so special. I wiped Isaiah's face with the coarse paper, and he squirmed away from me.

'Stop,' he howled. I dipped a fry in ketchup to placate him. We sat long after we were done in our chairs, stunned by the weight in our bellies.

'C'mon,' I said eventually. 'I got the bottles.'

I arranged them in a line at the base of the dining-room door, first the green one and then the two blue ones. Isaiah squatted down beside me, both hands on his knees.

'It's going to be okay now,' I said.

He reached for my hand, slipping his into mine. His thumb went into his mouth for comfort. I picked him up to draw him away from that door. It had followed me down Flatbush, across Ocean, through 18th and down along Newkirk. I had seen it looming always in the back of my mind, tall and flimsy, made from plywood with a cheap brass doorknob that swung loosely when I locked it. The sound of the laboring air conditioner behind it had haunted me, hiccuping and switching gears, trying to live up to the demands placed upon it. I couldn't see what was on the other side of that door, but even as I played go fish with Isaiah, confident that nothing could cross that barrier of blue glass, I imagined that everything on the other side of it had gone black, the sheet-covered body on the table sucking out all of the room's light. ■

Gboyega Odubanjo

Census

good morning.

                **as you say. did you wake
well?**

when were you born?

                i was born in the afternoon.

there are many names
registered here. how many
names do you have?

                **well, thank god i am not
nameless.**

yes but how many?

                **i can't say there are too
many and i can't say there are
too few. it is god that gives.**

three or four?

                **is four too many? how many
have you?
so i can be sure.**

my names are in the records
for you to see.

                can i see them now?

you have to book an
appointment.

                when may i come?

a snake got into our office. it
has eaten our records. when
they have retrieved my name
it can be sent to you.

don't worry. the snake has
been dealt with.

it is as god wills.

how many names sir? should
we want to honour you. so that
we know how much stone is
needed.

honour me as i am.
it is as god wills.

and how many has god willed
for you?

should one count names like
goats? is that not pride? will
those without not cuss me?

what is your government name?

i have no government. all the
names i have seen have been
lists. all the lists are dead and
incomplete.

it would allow us to correctly
identify you.

identify me for what?
i have not entered any lottery.

should your people need you.

well. say some names and
eventually i will come.

Courtesy of the author

VARIATIONS

Tao Lin

The next day, Li typed, 'Feel closer to Kay today than any day so far.' At night, Kay texted saying she was home from visiting her mom, whom she visited on Sundays. She asked if Li wanted to get his glasses, which were in her room, or if she should bring them.

Li asked if she wanted to hang out.

'I do. Maybe just for a little bit?'

Li went to her room at 7.15 p.m. They decided to part at 8.30, set an alarm for 8.30, and had sex twice. Kay said while biking home from the Upper West Side, where her mom lived, she'd thought that she wouldn't see Li until Friday. She'd also thought she wouldn't plan anything, and that Li had been obsessed with the Hutchison Effect but then had seemed to lose interest. What if that happened with her?

Li said he'd learned of Hutchison the previous month, but had known Kay for four years, and that he was still interested in Hutchison but had gotten more interested in glyphosate recently because it directly affected his body. He'd learned from MIT researcher Stephanie Seneff that glyphosate was embedded in his collagen, receptors and other proteins – in his eyes, hands, face, brain and heart – because life mistook the herbicide for glycine when building proteins.

His ongoing, deepening realization that he was very damaged

compared to his ancestors from centuries, millennia and especially tens of millennia ago was a reliable source of encouragement: even with all the damage, there were times of startling clarity and poignant mystery, moments to weeks of serenity, harmony and happiness.

Kay said it would be okay if Li lost interest in her. They listened to Glenn Gould's extremely fast, 1955 recording of Bach's thirty-variation Goldberg Variations. Kay's mom, who owned a piano, had gotten Kay the sheet music, which Kay felt was surprisingly difficult due to its rhythm. The 8.30 alarm went off.

The next night, they decided to meet from 7.30 to 9 p.m., a variation of the previous night. In 3A, Kay asked Li to teach her a stretch. They did 'dry swimming'.

They went to Li's fire escape, where they looked at a green-lit Empire State Building and considered what had transpired since it was red, six days earlier.

Kay asked Li where in America seemed to him like a good place to live. Li said Hawaii. Kay agreed and said her friend Diane's brother lived in Kauai, where he earned money by running a rental.

One of the trees by the fire escape had the Yoshida Effect, with a bifurcating trunk. Kay said she'd told her brother about the effect, and he'd said, 'Isn't that just a normal feature of trees?' Li said the Yoshida Effect was as important to him as the Hutchison Effect, or more. 'I like variation #2 a lot,' Kay texted after they parted.

The next night, in variation #3, they ate a cheese-avocado omelet, delayed parting thrice, and spent three hours together. Li learned Kay had all thirty-two of her teeth, and Kay said she felt both calm and excited around him. 'It's 11.18 and I keep thinking of Kay,' typed Li after they parted.

In 3A two nights later, he found himself unpleasantly daydreaming about the end of their relationship, distracting himself into quiet glumness. Before parting, they talked about Kay feeling overwhelmed at work, and Li suggested she write a book. 'Feel weirdly detached,' he typed in 4K. 'Maybe we could spend less time together. Or see each other when we're not tired.'

The next day, he canceled dinner with out-of-town friends. 'For some reason, I was critical and gloomy last night,' he typed. 'I kept suspecting Kay of doing things to get me to like her more. Seems insane. I should be alone when like that.' He stared out the window, past autumning foliage, at the brick building. 'There's no need to feel bad about losing or changing interest. It could lead to better things.'

But in variation #5 they spent ten hours together. On the A train, they bought a drawing of four flowers, three clouds, two trees and one ground for one dollar from an androgynous child going car-to-car seemingly alone, selling art from a folder labeled 'Positive Energy Project'. At a Renaissance fair, Li said he liked that Kay had a career, because he also had things to do; his previous girlfriends had had part-time jobs at most. Kay asked if he'd recorded her since 12 August in Stuyvesant Square Park. Li said he hadn't and wouldn't. Kay thanked him and said he could, if he wanted; it wasn't illegal.

In #6, they started a book club and agreed they were addicted to each other. After #7, Li excitedly emailed himself while hanging upside down on his pull-up bar, 'I felt we were doomed five days ago, but now I feel the opposite.' In #8, Kay said she hadn't been around her mom, who 'wasn't good at night', for more than a day in maybe ten years. Li talked about getting massaged, seeing a chiropractor and going to a physical rehabilitation center in Taiwan a year and a half earlier.

In #9, a sleepover at Kay's, they read some of the Nicholson Baker novel *Vox*, their first book club choice. In bed, Li learned Kay had a pet snail in kindergarten named Emily who ate lettuce and watermelon. Snails seemed Daoist to Li – mellow, unrushed, at home anywhere. To Kay, they seemed brave, decisive, strong-willed and resilient. As a last resort, snails could self-reproduce; selfing produced fewer eggs and fewer surviving hatchlings than mating.

In #10, they drank coffee together for the first time, generating a somewhat tense discussion regarding Amazon.com. Li wanted to discuss its unobvious positives. He'd found *Cure Tooth Decay*, *Surviving Evil* and other illuminating books there that most media didn't cover and weren't in most bookstores. They decided to say 'Amazon' to refer to the jungle five times per time they referenced the corporation. Kay said it would be good if they had as many variations as there were bird species in the Amazon.

They biked around the Lower East Side, visiting a bookstore, two parks and two gardens. In Union Square, they made plans to fast, organize a Joy Williams conference and make raw-milk ice cream. Li had been ordering raw-milk goods, including yogurt and cheese, from a company that his friend Rainbow had told him about that delivered from farms in New Jersey. Most people were allergic to pasteurized milk, a relatively recent invention, but not raw or fermented milk, he'd read in *The Untold Story of Milk*.

In 4K, they got Kay's period blood on Li's sofa during sex, and Li praised the natural substance, saying it was a welcome presence in his nature-deficient, virtual-reality-like room. Holding each other, they reviewed their day aloud, taking turns chronologically describing what happened.

They watched an autism documentary that made Li feel sad and frustrated, then sat in Washington Square Park. Li began to feel better while telling Kay that he'd added tobacco, which he'd begun smoking with cannabis in an 80–20 cannabis-tobacco mix, and snails to his book – in a sentence on how snails and other animals had kept living in an eternal-seeming, cyclical trance when humans entered history, and a sentence on how Indigenous people had enjoyed pesticide-and-additive-free tobacco (smoking it, snuffing it and drinking it as a tea or in ayahuasca) for millennia.

In the morning, they decided to visit Hawaii together soon, then ate eggs and parted. Walking home from the library five hours later, ruminating on the previous night, Li felt himself turning against their relationship – he was trying to leave New York, while Kay, who liked slowness but seemed deep into fast society, working sixty-plus hours a week for a demanding boss, seemed to be settling in, with a new job and apartment and her mom in the city – but the uncontrollable-seeming thoughts dispersed when he got home, read a text from Kay and got stoned.

In 3A the next day, they made and ate lemongrass-arugula omelets. Li said he used to be bloated and have pain and discomfort most of the time. He'd assumed he was weaker than other people. Kay said she'd always blamed herself for being slow. Li said he didn't think she was slow, but that she just had a lot to do, and she went to work.

In the park, editing a printed draft of his novel's 'Florida' chapter, in which he family-vacationed for five days in Orlando, Li thought about the mystery. It seemed to be almost everything – every life form, dream, thought and emotion. It was everywhere except where it was obscured by culture or technology – sitcoms, advertisements, skyscrapers, smartphones. 'The mystery is Kay and me in bed naked imagining us as complex squirrels looking at each other's faces,' wrote Li on his paper.

He considered the secret. It increasingly seemed to be 'Nothing at all is what it appears to be,' as ethnobotanist Kathleen Harrison had said in a 2015 talk. 'And I have learned that in my many years not only from taking psychedelics but of working with native peoples who seem to understand that much better than our materially oriented cultures do – that "everything is an illusion and everything may change from what it appears to be now to something else at any moment" is kind of a rule to live by.'

Kay texted, 'I think I'm accidentally stoned.' Li realized they'd used the coffee grinder he used for cannabis on the lemongrass that morning for their omelets and that being unwittingly more stoned than normal had led to thoughts on mystery and secrets. He apologized and asked Kay what she was going to do. She said she was in her apartment, reading; she'd told her boss she had a migraine.

Three days later, Li's divorce confirmation arrived early, freeing him to leave epicentral society. Teaching and pain had kept him there in 2014 and 2015, the nonfiction book and divorce in 2016 and that year. 'One of my first thoughts was that I don't want to leave anymore because of Kay,' he typed in his notes.

At city hall, he turned in a card to confirm receipt of the confirmation. In a nearby plaza, lying on a strip of grass, breathing deeply while reading *Vox*, he went briefly unconscious. Returning to concrete reality, he realized with excitement and poignant wonder that he was still far from assimilating Kay into his life. He'd been alone for so long.

The next day, on the urban farm where Rainbow's girlfriend worked, Li and Kay put their hands into hot compost, played hide-and-seek and ate koji-fermented steak. On the way home, they entered a pinball arcade and discussed every machine. Before bed, they watched YouTube videos of *Kid Icarus* and other Nintendo games.

In the morning, they watched a talk on severe autism, which affected more than a million Americans. The talk included video of an autistic child's inflamed intestines, photos of boys who'd beaten themselves unconscious while trying to attack their swollen brains, and a home movie of an adult self-protectively wearing a football helmet, which reminded Li of psychic driving, an MKULTRA technique in which people were forced to hear the same statements half a million times from electronic helmets.

Society seemed to mainly pay attention to functional autists, whose mild symptoms, giving them new perspectives, could be viewed as desirable. Around half of US children with autism couldn't speak, though, according to the California Department of Education. A third had epilepsy – chronic brain seizures. A fourth harmed themselves. Many would never have a job or partner. Li hadn't ever been that autistic. For most of his life, he'd been borderline-to-mildly autistic. He was becoming gradually less autistic over years through nutrition, detoxification, practice and cannabis.

Li felt himself and Kay watching the talk with their full attention, as seemed to be their style. Days later, they'd learn they'd both cried.

Li asked if she wanted to watch more. She said no; she wanted to work. She worked at home on Mondays. Li lay stomachdown on a stomachdown Kay and joked it was a strategy to keep her in his room.

She said he didn't need to lie on her for that.

He accompanied her to 3A, returned to 4K and typed notes. Since their kiss a month earlier, time had felt faster. His relationship with his mom had been saner and friendlier. His inflammation had regularly reached new lows, which made sense because he'd severely lacked social contact, in-person friendship, hugs, kisses, sex and other anti-inflammatory, immune-enhancing human trademarks for four years.

In 4K two nights later, they ate six types of eggplant. Kay's eyes seemed darker and more charged than Li had ever seen them as she talked about psychotherapy, which she'd had at 6.30 a.m. 'Deranged?' she said. 'No,' said Li. 'I liked it.' Kay had started therapy, in which she mostly discussed her mom and work, two months earlier on a recommendation from her brother and was considering stopping. She said talking about therapy had begun to 'feel like a schtick'.

She said the previous night, unable to sleep, she'd read an article titled 'Fertility Awareness, Food, and NightLighting' and realized her menstrual pains and irregular cycle were healable. The article was by Katie Singer, the author of *An Electronic Silent Spring*. They decided to read *The Garden of Fertility*, Singer's book on fertility awareness, a method of charting temperature, cervical fluid and cervix changes to prevent pregnancy naturally, next in their book club.

The next night, they ate cannabis, walked to Carnegie Hall, sat on the fifth floor, and watched an orchestra play Verdi's sinfonia from *Aida*. Martha Argerich appeared and sat at a piano. Prokofiev's third piano concerto began.

After the first, quiet movement, Li began to feel increasingly worried, struggling to stifle hysterical laughter. Kay seemed to be laughing too.

Li walked past five people to the aisle and left the hall, laughing. Kay appeared twenty seconds later. They listened to the softened, clarified concerto from the lobby.

Walking home, they discussed their first times having sex (both in college in their first relationships), her birth-control history (the pill from 2001 to 2011, causing hair loss, dry hands, weight gain and a darkened face), porn (he used to be addicted to it; she'd only seen it in passing – the idea to find and watch porn had never occurred to her, she said, which made Li laugh) and that it seemed good and rare that they hadn't had alcohol together.

In bed in 4K, falling asleep with Kay spooning him from behind, Li bristled with startlingly unambiguous love. ■

3 issues of
Prospect for just £1!

Plus, receive a free copy of
Shuggie Bain by Douglas Stuart (RRP £14.99)

**Prospect* is perfect for those who want:*

to be the first to **understand the big ideas** that are shaping our world

independent thinking and debate— you won't find the party line here

in-depth analysis on the big issues by **the world's best writers**

Your free gift

An uncompromising yet warmly witty exploration of love, pride and poverty, *Shuggie Bain* charts the endeavours of its eponymous protagonist—an ambitious and fastidious boy from a dire mining town with a thirst for a better life. A blistering debut by a brilliant writer with an important story to tell.

AMY KEY
Agnes, 2020

A PLACE I'D GO TO

Kathryn Scanlan

It sat at the crotch, so to speak, of the spread-eagled strip mall. Out front was a cramped rhombus of fake grass tamped into a depression of concrete which – inch for inch – must've been one of the more pissed-upon places of the Earth.

Behind the reception desk there'd be some odorous soupy dish or goopy dip in a takeout tray, two or three half-drunk plastic cups of melted iced coffee, and several ripped sacks of scattered snacks. The receptionist was a young woman in a hoodie with unwashed hair and one perpetually red, infected eye.

The office cat was a fat gray stray with a missing leg. It sat in its basket of dirty towels next to the credit-card machine and rubbed its cold, wet nose on your hand while you signed your receipt. The cat liked to be patted firmly on the back, in the dander-powdered crook of the tail.

On the walls were garish paintings and boring photographs of pets, hung salon-style in big gaudy gold frames. Tall patrons knocked their heads against a low-slung plastic chandelier. Others sat on hot-pink padded chairs with their ill, anxious companions and spoke to them in squeaky baby voices or the booming, condescending theatrics of people performing parenthood in public.

The animals trembled and some tried to hide under the furniture.

They'd been vomiting or were vomiting still. They'd been attacked by one of their kind or hit by a car. Their teeth were rotting and their hair was falling out. They had cancer and diabetes and urinary tract infections. Their hearts were full of worms. They were very old and had to be carried down the hall to the examination room and lifted onto and off the scale like sacks of tender, bruisable fruit.

When I spoke to my pet, I spoke at a volume only she could hear. But she was mostly deaf and if anything she felt it – my low, unremarkable rumble.

I went to this place once a month, twice a month – then once a week, twice a week. I bought vials of eye ointment and eye drops, ear ointment and ear drops, little pain pills and big ones, pills for inflammation, diarrhea and pulmonary hypertension, and small tubs of bacon-flavored pill putty. I kept it all arranged on a tray at home, on top of the dryer in my laundry room. I chopped up the white and blue and pink pills with a razor blade into halves, quarters, eighths and sixteenths, then wrapped them in putty or crushed them into a slurry with gravy or whipped them with yogurt or tinned ground buffalo organs.

Then – one day – I no longer needed to go there. I no longer needed the vials or putty or buffalo pâté, though I had plenty left. The little shattered pills I'd prepared in advance sat on their tray. Dust fell gently onto them.

I suddenly had so much time I felt I might fall into it, as my pet had. From this chute – which opens and shuts quickly, sneakily, like a carnivorous plant – nothing is ever recovered.

I started making trips to the grocery store when my cupboards were already packed with food. I stopped for gas with a full tank and checked my adequately pressurized tires. At Doodads Etcetera I sniffed each scented candle on offer though I hate scented candles and would never buy one.

Driving home from a dried-bean shop one afternoon, I spotted the strip mall I'd spent so much time in and made an abrupt left into the lot. Inside, the funky, familiar odor was there to greet me. The three-legged cat stood up, stretched and offered its rump for a pet. The red-eyed receptionist sucked pale coffee through a straw. She got to the bottom of the cup – then the cup was empty. She tossed it into a trash can under her desk. I'd never seen one of her coffees come to an end before now and hadn't believed she ever actually finished them. My life is full of stupid revelations like this one and if you stick around I will tell you some more. ■

SOFT PINK LIGHT

Kaitlin Maxwell

Introduction by Lynne Tillman

Kaitlin Maxwell is daughter and granddaughter to the two women in this series. Maxwell appears with them in some pictures, imitating or mimicking their poses, wearing the same costumes. She shoots them alone, shoots herself alone, she poses them against different backgrounds, mostly domestic spaces, but not only. Maxwell's images represent an intense curiosity about them, the women who raised her, about who they are, apart from her, and who she is because of them. Maxwell wants to know if she looks like them.

Nine and six years younger than my two sisters, I watched them as I grew up. They fascinated me. From my bed, I watched my middle sister put on her bra on a freezing winter morning, and felt sorry for her – I wore an undershirt, but a bra wouldn't keep her warm. They were my brilliant sisters, my heroes, until they were not.

My mother, the first female, was a 'prude'. Our female bodies were not talked about, they were our secrets; what happened to them, and what we did with them, was secret. We didn't walk around naked. My father's body was also kept under wraps. When my breasts started growing, I thought the small mounds, or lumps, might be a disease.

*

Maxwell's images are revelatory to me, unusual: she looks at her close female relatives as characters in their bodies, with bodies. Daughter and granddaughter, she seeks ways of seeing them, and to perceive femininity, sensuality, sexuality and 'sexiness' in them and her, and also as coded images. That is, she depicts all of this as 'just pictures' of women. Her mother and grandmother are shown as sensual, voluptuous, while the archetypical 'Mother' is not. Good-looking, fit women, they pose, and don't; they reveal their bodies, and don't.

The poses and postures of 'femininity' and 'womanhood' supply part of Maxwell's material. Simone de Beauvoir famously wrote, women aren't born, they are made. (I love Aretha, but don't believe there's a 'natural-born woman'.) And, the concept of 'natural' changes over time, indicating that so-called 'natural behaviors' also change, or that nothing is natural. Females will be inculcated, educated, indoctrinated with how to look; how to get looked at; how to behave, and what they can expect of life 'as women'.

In photography, the knowledge that pictures are constructed, that they are in some sense always fictional – that is, made up – has troubled and wounded the medium. A photograph can't assert itself as a fact or document. Because like the humans who invented the medium, photographs can dissemble and shape-shift. It is this understanding among photographers that presents a great dilemma: they assemble or frame or construct an image that already is an image, and already seen.

When I was seven, I saw Marilyn Monroe in the movie *Niagara*. I don't know who took me. In one scene, Marilyn appeared in a tight-fitting, low-cut fuchsia dress. I had never seen anyone like her. She was sexy. I sent away to her Hollywood studio for an autographed picture. It was the only time I ever did that. It was a little black-and-white picture of her in a bathing suit. She was smiling, posed high on her toes, standing in profile, and looked cute and friendly, I thought.

Monroe became an object of fascination to me, a baby feminist. Her performance of sexuality startled me. Was I supposed to be like that or only admire images of women like that. In the early 1980s, I tried to write her autobiography, to write as Marilyn Monroe, tell her story intimately, but after reading what had been published about her, I became too depressed to write it – her early life was miserable – and, in the 1990s I turned what I had written into 'Dead Talk', a short story about Marilyn.

Animals flirt, give off signals for mating; male birds do elaborate dances, their colors brighten and shimmer; some males fight to the death for a female, and sometimes an animal merely rubs against a tree or sprays leaves to lay down its scent. Marilyn Monroe's flamboyant dress, her exaggerated stroll, her ass in perpetual movement modeled one version of the female of my species using vivid, revealing costumes to catch a mate.

In this Western world, it's a toss-up. Sometimes it's the job of females to attract partners; perfume can be used as scent. Men often appear not to need prompts; they were bred to play the aggressor. (They have image problems, also.) Too passive, they may not get what they want. Too aggressive, they might frighten their target. Some are predatory.

In several of her photographs, Maxwell's women strike poses that might be considered sexy or provocative. These replications are studies in sexiness.

In the first image of the series, Maxwell faces the camera, its remote device on her lap, and shoots from there. She is sitting on a stool in jeans and a black bra, beside a yellow stove. Her legs open into a V and mimic the V of the corner behind her back. The kitchen's yellow wallpaper, the background, denotes its era, the 1950s or 1960s.

(My immediate association to seeing the yellow wallpaper was a story, 'The Yellow Wallpaper', by Charlotte Perkins Gilman in 1892. A woman is suffering a terrible, post-partum depression, and kept in a room – a cage, a prison – with yellow wallpaper.)

Maxwell shows herself in a homely, dated environment. The photographer makes herself a target, boldly central in the frame. She is also to be investigated. Later, as the series progresses, Maxwell will contrast this homeliness to her mother's and grandmother's versions of domesticity and the feminine.

Voluptuous bodies wear casual or revealing clothes. The women appear not to mind being shot; Maxwell herself seems more tense or, as the photographer, less comfortable in front of the camera. Maybe the women were uncomfortable, they just know how to perform. A viewer can't tell. Poses are performances, and Maxwell's photographs are not didactic, yet one could decide that, through her photographs, she is depicting a girl's education of learned 'womanliness', and how to do it. 'Strike a pose.'

She uses bright light, natural light, shadow or low light to build moods, feelings – openness, secrecy, obscurity, ambiguity. She mostly foregrounds her subjects, while the background embraces them – the women appear to have a place, in a place. But Maxwell frames her subjects as if an actual border were surrounding them.

She uses color subtly, often pastels.

Her pictures mostly work with a few elements, and not extraneous information. There's overhead light in a bathroom scene, where her grandmother applies lipstick. Maxwell has shot her from an angle. We see her in profile, and also, her full face in a mirror, one side of which is bright, the other dim. The mirror she looks into is divided.

In Maxwell's images, women mirror each other. Maxwell lies in bed, part of her body under covers, while her grandmother lies, curled on the floor in a shift dress. In two other shots, similar poses are struck by Maxwell with her mother, and with her grandmother.

In the first, Maxwell and her mother stand side by side in a backyard, an old wood fence behind them. The mother's head leans toward her daughter's, and both are wearing black pants, casual tops. They look at the camera, they look 'ordinary'.

In the other, Maxwell and her grandmother stand in front of a white garage door, next to each other but not touching. Her grandmother is wearing a low-cut black sleeveless dress that reveals her large breasts. Maxwell wears a see-through top, her smaller breasts peeking through the interstices of the netting. Both women have angled their legs, as models do to present a slimmer image.

Dueling images, let's say, juxtapositions within juxtapositions, facing each other.

*

Apart from her formal concerns, Maxwell's content – femininity, gender, sexuality, women as constructions, representations and self-representation, mothers, daughters – are compound(ed) subjects, not separable in her pictures. To represent females and their bodies is a thorny job. Any one issue engages others. 'Motherhood' is a construction, and its representations of maternity shape ideas about how a mother should look and act. A mother is also an image – but whose.

Women look at women, men look at women, straight, queer, non-binary individuals look at women – looking is complex.

I'm recalling Laura Mulvey's seminal essay on classic cinema's 'look' and 'gaze' at women, a function of patriarchy, control by men of women, particularly in a narrative, which breeds in women an internalized male gaze. (Recently, Mulvey has said she understands her seminal essay as a manifesto, as polemical.)

A woman is looking at other women, she gazes at them, and herself, she makes pictures of all. Viewers look through her lens, her eye. So, as a viewer, I can only project, which is what I am doing. My responses or interpretations, my seeing, get filtered through my psychology, my associations. My curiosity stems from a desire to apprehend the psychological moment in them, and how and why Maxwell's work produces or promotes certain stories.

I don't know if I can see, separate from my gender, the ideas I have unconsciously absorbed. I don't think I'm a woman. Consciousness awakens one to inherited or educated biases. That is my hope. I might be able to see as a queer woman or straight man, say. Or, I might be caged in my own room of yellow wallpaper. I can't claim a clean sweep of that room's indoctrinations, my early education, can't say it's been done thoroughly or completely. Making formal analyses helps me, I think, see other ways than subjectively to see, but still . . .

I suppose I want to find a coherent narrative, and know I will not. Questions have been around for a long while: if female bodies are represented by women, are they any different from those shot or painted by men? Maxwell's photographs dive into these muddy waters in visual monologues and dialogues.

Photography's virtue is its vice: a seeming, immediate clarity – what you see is what you get – hides its truer illegibility.

One day, while writing this, I turned on the radio for background noise, which fills in for something, maybe an absence of ideas. It's a woman's voice. 'My husband thinks I'm obsessed with my breasts.' She's written a book about women's breasts, the American obsession with breasts since the Second World War. I can guess what she's going to say, and turn off the radio to wrestle with how to write about breasts in Maxwell's pictures; they figure prominently, under clothes or partly unclothed. I might be looking at their breasts the way a man would.

Maxwell seems to be comparing and contrasting her body and their bodies. In one photograph, she wears the same costume as her grandmother. Their breasts are exposed in the same way, just above the midriff of their lingerie.

The first time my mother mentioned breasts to me, I was five and with her at a beach club my family had joined. An elderly woman in a bathing suit passed by; she had extremely large breasts that hung down almost to her waist. My mother, who was not 'busty', said: 'It's good to have small breasts so that doesn't happen when you're old And then your back won't hurt.' She never said anything like that again.

Toward the end of the series, Maxwell presents two suggestive, ambiguous and puzzling works, disconcerting in ways her other photographs or scenes are not, and they are of herself – self-portraits. She is sitting at the edge of a bed, fairly close up, and wearing a red plaid shirt. Blood is dripping from her nose; a hand is raised almost shoulder level, one finger also bloody. Her face seems naked, surprised, upset, shocked. She appears to have been crying.

It took me a while to recognize her bloody nose. (I think it is a bloody nose, I have had bloody noses.) This pose, and why she is showing us it, suggests many responses, and I find myself associating wildly. First, blood and women, menstruation and other bodily functions. But the blood forms a straight line from her nose down to her chin, then across her upper lip, forming a cross; the way she is holding her hand up and cupped, with two fingers raised more than the others – this, I think, mines religious imagery. Stigmata, stigma, a sign of disgrace.

The photograph's ambiguity allows, encourages, sensitive or harsh readings – for one, women's shame about their bodies. Not all women, not in all societies, not all at all. This shame is mostly a hidden terrain, and contemporary women are supposed to be over it. If only.

A woman can feel shame about her vagina. Vagina dentata! She might be embarrassed about having her period, or the 'curse'. (My mother never used that term; she also never told me about periods, I sent away for pamphlets.) Come menopause, this woman will be told she's no longer attractive, here's room on the shelf. Controlling weight, that fixation to be skinny, functions as a way to submerge these other feelings, to control the body. It's an illusion, but an all too common one. Her body is trouble. The stigma is to be a woman.

Maxwell has set her final scene – a self-portrait – in a pink bathroom, with pink tiles, in soft pink light, pink towels on a rack. The background is in soft focus. Maxwell wears a delicate pink bra and pink half-slip, and is seated on top of a toilet seat. Her hair is pulled up neatly in a bun; she is looking at the camera at an angle, not facing it, the remote again in her lap.

Maxwell's look at the camera, at the viewer, seems significant, and different from the other self-portraits. She might be peeking at us, exposing herself. Setting it in a bathroom, she has invaded a private realm. The photograph acknowledges she is doing this, exposing herself and her mother and grandmother. Maxwell has taken liberties, and recognises that she is invading their privacy with her pictures of intimate relationships. She also reminds viewers of their/our common bodily functions.

This picture is beautiful, I think, though its setting might read as unglamorous. It's a compelling picture, for one, because of Maxwell's gaze, a question rests in it, and also defiance, and yet a sense of serenity. Maybe a feeling of completion for her.

This final picture cannily returns us to the beginning, to her first photograph, another self-portrait. Maxwell is in a kitchen, sitting next to a yellow stove. She starts the sequence with yellow and ends it with pink. It's a soft landing. ■

AESTHETICA

CREATIVE WRITING AWARD 2021

SUBMIT

YOUR WRITING TODAY

**POETRY
FICTION**

**WIN £5000
& PUBLICATION**

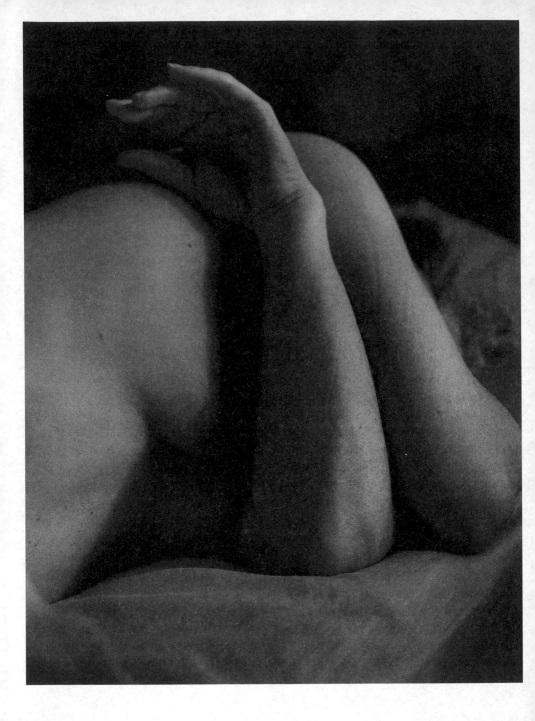

RAYMOND MEEKS

TIDES

Sara Freeman

On the long bus journey out, she doesn't cry or even have a single thought that she can name. She watches the dark impossibility of the road instead, the mostly empty seats ahead of her, the head of a woman a few rows up, listing forward and then jolting back. She does not sleep. She wants to be awake to make her declaration at the border. She will show her passport and when they ask, *Where to?* she will say without hesitation, *The sea.*

She does not have to leave. No one says: *You must go.* No clothes thrown out the window, no eviction notice. Her husband is already gone by then; she was the one to tell him that he had to go. She could say it was the baby – her brother's and his wife's. His sweet squawking through the open window in the apartment beneath hers. She could no longer live in this fixed way: their joy so firmly lodged beneath her grief. She could say that.

The motel advertises an ocean breeze but is nowhere near the beach. She waits in the small room, for something, for someone. She has turned her phone off, but she still feels it in her palm, waiting to bleat back to life. To deliver what message? *I love you. I miss you. Come back.* She left a note for her brother and his wife. No explanation or apology. *I'll be fine!* That's what she wrote. She asks at the reception desk about another motel, nearer the water this time. The woman behind the counter has eyebrows like tadpoles swimming lazily across her forehead. She says there is a town she might like, remote, for rich folks mostly, about thirty miles up the coast. There is a hostel there too. She puts her index finger on a map, her nail filed down to a tidy point. This one is canary yellow, the surrounding ones sky blue.

She gets a ride from a man who is delivering ice across the state. His eyes are blue and inflamed, his hands raw and meaty. The town sign reads: THIS ROAD LEADS TO ROME, with an ugly drawing of the Colosseum, followed by the population, 2,353. When she gets out in the town's central square, she touches the hard shell of the truck with gratitude and it is so cold, the hairs on her arm stand up.

There is no coliseum in this Rome. Instead, a supermarket, a Greek restaurant, an Italian restaurant, a seafood spot, an ice-cream shop, a wine store, a laundromat, a pub, an inn, a garden center, a health center, a hardware store, a library, a clothing store, a pharmacy, a marina and a dump.

The sea, in this new town, is surprisingly hard to get to. It is somehow everywhere and nowhere. She needs an invitation, a private viewing: through the stately homes, and onto the other side, where everything is vast and pristine. The other her, the one she left behind, would have easily slid between the giant piles, past the outdoor furniture, past the slim lounging bodies and their pure-bred dogs. Everything belonged to her then; that was back when she believed that nothing that could so easily be had wasn't somehow already hers.

From her bedroom window in the hostel, she can see it best: the sea and its expanse, edging in and then pulling back. She doesn't want to be in it yet. It is warm out, but she still feels frozen, blood-let, fleshless. She is content, for now, to watch the comings and goings from afar.

*

In the evenings, she walks along the town's main drag. It is shaped like a horseshoe. She often sees the same faces twice, on the way to the ice-cream shop, and then on their way back. There are often tears on the return journey, mostly children's, but on one occasion a grown woman's and her wife's. Once desire is met, she thinks, there is only turning back from it. There is not much to do or see in the town at night: just tourists dining al fresco, prodding swordfish slabs and slurping oysters. A busker nearby crooning, *Oh, oh, Mexico*, as if he might be in this town in error. The first nights, she stops and finds a place among the small crowd gathered before him. But one evening, mid-song, he looks up and greets her with a complicit nod. Now, when she hears the busker's familiar sound, she passes by without so much as looking up.

She asks around at the hostel, and they tell her she is right: the prettiest beaches are cut off by the houses. It wasn't always like this, they say, the coastline so private and all. Some of the richest families used to turn a blind eye, but not anymore. In a few weeks, once the season is over, then that's a whole different story. For now there's the public beach, of course, but that's nothing to write home about. That's good, because she's not planning to write home about anything. They laugh, hearing her say this, and she thinks for a moment that nothing much has changed: she can say a few words in the right order and get people to love her for a moment.

She finds it, flanked by the supermarket and the garden center: a slip of public sand. There is an orange tent set up at the far end of the beach and two pairs of swollen, mangled feet sticking out. When she walks by, the screen is zipped halfway down, so that she can't see any faces, she can only hear the syncopated sound of their snoring.

She wonders what she will do when the money runs out. The thought is sticky, the first one like this, insisting on its own importance. It seems absurd somehow, that she must think of it, make something of this thought. The beach ends and there is a large expanse of dark, jagged rocks. She walks across the fraught ground, canvas shoes sliding dangerously beneath her. She slips and catches herself then slips again and falls hard on the rock. Not pain, just the feeling of everything coming up from within. She sits there, looking around, for someone, a witness to her fall, a hand to grip as she steadies herself back up. But there is no one, just the dome of orange light tented in the distance.

She buys a large lemonade filled with crushed ice and drinks it until her teeth and brain are numb. She shuts her eyes hard and when she opens them again, she is surprised to find that everything is still there: the lemonade truck, a few waves quietly churning in the distance, the sand, dank and gray, waiting to be touched.

She wakes one morning, clutching her stomach. No time has passed; her husband is by her side. He touches her rounded stomach with his palm. *Nearly there,* he says, speaking into her belly button. She is awake now, her palm on her own skin, the fingers cold and thin. Her belly is nearly concave, more than empty. She has been gone for three days, maybe four, or maybe it is six, and since then she has eaten a sleeve of saltines, some peanut butter from a spoon, a few beers, a lemonade, some fries and some licorice. She is saving money; she doesn't have much left. One thousand seven hundred and thirty-three. If she needs more, she'll turn the phone on, write her brother a message. He has never said no to her before. His only sister. She'll write to him and say something like this: *I am changing.* Or better yet: *I have changed.*

She sees children everywhere, in the flesh, but also in what they leave behind: striped swimsuits hanging over banisters and beach chairs, colorful pails discarded on the beach. When she sees them, children and their traces, she turns her head away. It is her head that does the turning. She speaks, as though defending herself before a jury: *This* is not about *that.*

*

At the town's small marina, day trippers clump around the seafood spot, composing their seaside shots: plush pink lobster rolls, heaped French fries snapped from above. In the background, a row of handsome wooden yachts, sterns wagging; a fisherman, sun-creased and smoking, unloading his mid-August catch. She doesn't stay long; the smell here makes her queasy. Fish entrails and sunscreen, cooking oil reused one time too many.

In a shop window along the main drag, she spots a letterpress sign: KEEP ROME OFF THE MAP. In this town, the patrician crowd don their modesty like a crown: beat-up station wagons, worn-in khakis, styles from thirty years past.

The diner here is famous for its 1950s memorabilia. She sits at the counter and orders the lumberjack special. She pictures a lumberjack laying her across his lap, breaking her, like a twig, in half. She eats a sausage link and one of three sunny-side-up eggs, a bit of the pancake just for the mouthful of syrup. This diner, with its defunct Coke machines and jukeboxes and old graphic lunchboxes, reminds her of her mother's house, crammed with dangerous nostalgia. A woman and her toddler sit nearby. She spoons cereal into his wet little mouth. He dribbles and she wipes. He dribbles and she wipes. Easy as that. The woman is wearing all linen and a large-brimmed hat; she looks old to be a mother. But who is she to say who is old and who is not? She was thirty-five when she got pregnant, thirty-six when she lost her child. And now she feels one hundred, or maybe only seven years old. She looks a moment too long. Something passes between them, the mother and her, a warm current of it: pity, or maybe its cousin, contempt. When she asks for the bill the man at the counter, pointing to the table where the mother and son were sitting, says, *They said to say good luck.*

In the bathroom mirror, she lets herself look up. She sees what the woman must have seen: the gaunt face, the hair matted to one side, the lips chapped, the nails bitten to the quick. She splashes cold water on her face and pulls her hair back. She looks nearly dead. *This* is not *that*. She looks down at her clothes; they are dirty but intact.

It is hot. The hottest day yet. August, slinking into September. Still hot by the evening, when the sun is a red face dipping its chin into the water. The public beach is empty. Everyone is on their patios sipping Campari and eating pistachios, saying their farewells. She removes her canvas shoes, her jeans and shirt, and moves into the water – sharp and cold as a knife's edge. She swims out until, when she turns her head, she can no longer make out her clothes bundled up on the sand, just a single line of darkness in the background. The water is bitter now, the moon just a sliver in the night, barely any comfort at all. She is that sliver, she thinks, drowning in the dark. She could die here, so slight and sinking. Nothing but her body to buoy her up. Whatever reserves she had, she has lost them now. She feels a rush of heat around her, her own urine, terror at her own thoughts. She thrashes around, trying to turn back, but even this turning, this changing course, seems impossible: the body has forgotten how to lead. It takes an eternity to move against the current, the arms and legs dumb with disuse and then too much exertion. She kicks hard, and then softer, it is easier this way, without trying at all; she is moving forward and back, lulled by the waves. She is like this forever, until she hits something, a rock, and then her knees hit it too, and she finds that she can crawl. Beneath her, the hard, wet certainty of the ground. She manages to get to her feet, finds her clothes in their pile, falls asleep in a damp heap.

She wakes before the sun and sits up, stiff and cold. She has always wanted this: to slip beneath the surface, to dispossess herself. Now that she has done it, it is hard to remember how her self could have become such a bottomless pit: feed me, fuck me, fill me, love me.

This is what it feels like to slip, she remembers telling her husband, when she was teaching him to ice skate on the Ottawa canal. *You can't teach someone how to slip.* He was right: you slip and then you've slipped and so you know.

Sometimes, she pictures them: her brother and his wife, discussing her now that she is gone. *Impossible,* that's what they would say. Or maybe, instead, *beyond repair.*

The management has moved her things. *You were gone for two nights,* they tell her. She can only remember one, but she doesn't want to fight. Her things include: a toothbrush, a sweater, two T-shirts, one pair of jeans, the biography of a famous chef, all stuffed inside an old backpack with her brother's initials embroidered on it: P.S.T. They have placed her in the large dormitory. She can tell from the work boots neatly lining the beds that the place is full of men. She buys a six-pack of beer and some cigarettes and brings them with her to the beach. She will wait until the men are sleeping before climbing back into her cot. She lies down. The beer and cigarettes are effective; she feels herself drifting pleasantly into the night. Today she has only eaten half a packet of tea cookies and a banana. The waves are loud, brimming over, coursing to their violent meter. Before she falls asleep, she thinks: This is what babies must hear when they are held inside the womb.

She wakes to a hand on her shoulder, a gruff one, a man's hand, shaking her awake. A light so bright she can't make a thing out, only voices, two of them, ordering her to stand up. She is on the beach, her hand clutching at wet sand. Her eyes adjust and she sees them: two men in uniform. Father figures, she thinks. She smiles up at them. They don't smile back. Bad daddies. She says something out loud, but it sounds more garbled than what she had in her head. They grab her, one arm and then the other, not at the armpit, but by the wrists, as though she were just a kid. Swing me around and around and around and around. But it hurts, the joints are no longer loose; they are fixed in place. *You're hurting me,* she says, this time clearly. *I'm not doing anything wrong.* They point to the empty beer cans, more of them than she can remember drinking. She tries to explain: there were men in the hostel, she was just waiting for them to fall asleep. She is sitting in the back seat of their car now, hands cuffed. They have forgotten to put her seat belt on. The metal beneath the seat hits her tailbone, a familiar, pummeling beat. She has never been this cold, this brittle, her entire body caught up in a single spasm. *I'm still scared,* she says, at the door of the hostel: a giant mouth, gaping open. She begs the fat officer to take her inside, sit with her until she falls asleep, but he tells her, *Grow up, lady,* and takes his leave. Inside, all the men are sleeping, quiet as babies. She falls asleep quickly. When she wakes, she looks around and all the men are already gone.

The men are here for the season: blueberries, raspberries, blackberries. Three of them are working on a house. *The house is so big,* she hears one of them say in Spanish, *you could fit my whole village inside of it.*

They are kind, concerned for her. They say, *Güera, qué pasó?* pointing to her clothes, her shoes. She tells them, *Nada,* nothing has happened. They let her in on their talk. She likes being near them; she understands one in five words, this is enough.

She is like a ball being passed from one set of hands to another, none of them holding on for too long. In the communal kitchen, one offers her tortillas with beans, the other spaghetti from a can; another gives her cookies mortared with jam and vanilla cream. In the mornings, she wakes with them before dawn. They eat white bread slick with margarine, and make her Nescafé their special way: they heat the milk and let the granules dissolve, then add two heaping spoonfuls of sugar. The older one says: *Mija, tienes que comer,* and makes her eat a second piece of Wonder Bread sloppy with supermarket jelly.

One evening, she sees a few of the men huddled around the kitchen table, hunched over the cracked screen of a phone. In miniature, she makes out a penis sliding between two breasts as taut and playful as helium balloons. They turn the screen off as soon as they see her. They disperse, scatter back into the dormitory.

The young one asks her: *Cómo te llamas?* She tells him without much thought: *Nada.* She likes it as a name, *Nada.* The girls who work at the reception desk think it's strange: how much time she spends with the men, sitting and biting her nails, not talking at all. One morning, she finds her few clothes at the foot of her bed, folded and washed.

Sometimes, in the evenings, they watch a movie on the small television hanging from the ceiling. They all have to crane their necks to see the tiny men on the screen dangling from helicopters and saving women from burning buildings. Sometimes when she gets bored by the action, she walks around and picks up their empty beer cans, rinses them, arranges them neatly by the bin.

For the first time in her life, she does not dream.

In the middle of the night, she hears the young one in his bed. His moans are so low and muffled, she feels as though they are coming from her, a rush of blood in her own veins, a throbbing at her own throat. Not so long ago, she might have slipped out of bed, slid her hand between his legs and told him: *Let's try this instead.* The sound makes way for another, not sex but slow, withheld sobs, those of a much littler boy. Her body is stiff with remorse. She has no rounded edges anymore, no warmth to proffer him.

In the morning, she finds it hard to look at him. She pours him his cereal instead, his milk, dunks a spoon in it. *Aquí tienes.* He boasts about a girlfriend, a toddler back home. Two years, six months, three weeks and a day: this is how long it's been since he's seen them last. He is thick and strong and still growing, his front teeth too big for his mouth. She wants to touch the down on the upper lip and say, *There, there.*

*

She counts backward, tries to do her own dismal math. August, July, June, May, April, March. Five months since she saw her own child, eyes stuck shut, limp as an unclenched fist.

James Taylor is gone, but Joan Baez is there to replace him. She sings a song called 'Colorado', in which the only lyric is *Colorado*, repeated over and then over again. When she thinks the song is over, Joan begins again: *Colorado ... Colorado*. In Canada, where she is from, no one ever sings songs about Alberta.

The season is nearly done. She lets the fact of it wash over her. The city folks have gone home, the hostel will close. She hears it but the words are water and she a gripless surface, a flat expanse. The day arrives and the men are all packed up. *I miss you*, she tells them in Spanish. She doesn't know the future tense for *missing*. There is a van here to pick them up. She stands outside, nose running, waving, a single arm wrapped around her for warmth, a mother sending her boys off on the school bus.

The girls at the reception desk tell her she's got one day to clear out. They feel sorry for her, but they are only teenagers. *Senior year*, they say to her like a question and an answer all rolled into one. She tries to turn her phone back on, but the screen stays dark, every crevice filled with sand.

They tell her that if she helps them clean the place, she can stay three more nights. She vacuums and mops the floors, cleans the toilets and the scum between the tiles. She covers the furniture with tarps. She cleans the kitchen, consolidates all the half-eaten boxes of spaghetti into a single Ziploc bag. In the lost and found, she finds three dresses and two sarongs, a hot plate and a nightlight, an elegant fountain pen with the two parts of the nib violently split apart. The three of them collect 168 dollars' worth of coins, under the beds, inside the couches, in the laundry room under the machines. The girls whisper to one another and sheepishly offer her twenty dollars in dimes. She finds a lighter with a woman's silhouette on it. When it is upright, the woman wears a pretty pink dress. When she flips it upside down, the woman bares her ample breasts, a tassel, mid-twirl, on each nipple. During their lunch break, she sits in the sun and flips the lighter up and then down, up and then down again. The girls place a paper plate at her feet, a hot dog adorned with two perfect stripes: one red, one gold.

Three hundred and twenty-three dollars. This is counting the twenty dollars in dimes.

The three days are up. *Just one more night*, she begs. The girls hesitate, convene privately. *Fine*, they say, *but tomorrow morning you're gone, or else we're going to have to call the boss.* The next afternoon, they find her, still asleep in the cavernous room. *He's coming now*, they warn her. *He knows about you and he is displeased.* They use this word, *displeased*, as though it is a word she might not have heard before. They lay it on thick. They took a chance on her and now she's going to have to pay. She was their age once, sharpening herself against her own blunt force. And so she tells them she's very sorry, gives them fifty dollars, and buys them a six-pack each before taking her leave.

There are just hours left before sundown. Her backpack is heavy with hostel gleanings; the weight bears down on her shoulders, right down into her heels. Maybe she'll sleep on the public beach; she thinks of the tent, the mangled feet. She buys an ice-cream cone, soft vanilla sprinkled with a messy hand. She walks along the main street, not thinking, every mouthful too sweet. She takes inventory of her skills. The list is short and so, easy to remember.

That evening in the pharmacy, she buys soap, razors, shampoo and a cheap bottle of perfume. Mascara in a bright pink tube, a plum-red lipstick, foundation one grade of beige too dark – every item the cheapest she can find. She pays twenty dollars for a day pass at the health club. She asks how much for just a shower. *There's no price for that, miss.* She washes her hair, once, twice, three times, each strand stiffened with salt and grease. She looks down from time to time. She doesn't recognize the body beneath: feral, bleak. She shaves everything off. She forgot to ask for a towel so she walks around naked, drying herself off. She clips her nails and plucks her eyebrows, brushes her teeth. Two women in their sixties walk past her, catch a glimpse; she is denuded, goosebumped, a chicken with her feathers just off. They stare down sheepishly at her feet. She slips on one of the dresses from the hostel's lost and found. Floral, cheap. She is tall, and this spaghetti-strapped shift for someone shorter; it sits too high on her thighs. In the mirror, she sees what she will look like to others: she is not displeased. Only she knows what is amiss, like a loose tooth at the back of her mouth holding on by just a few threads. From time to time, she touches the fact of it with her tongue.

He is easy enough to spot. He orders a beer before the last one is halfway done. Rich boy, she thinks, hair smoothed back, gold pinky ring nestled in flesh. Prep school, financier, end-of-season loaf. She sits next to him. His teeth are small, his gums inflamed. He is already gone, left the building. She doesn't want money, she tells him, just a house to hole up in, a bed for the night. She takes his hand; she feels the fat pooling at the knuckles. She wonders if he ever takes the ring off, if he can. No, she doesn't do drugs, not that kind. *It's a real problem around here*, he says, in his newscaster's drone.

He is not a bad guy, she thinks, just a dummy, a clown. The ice clanks against his teeth, the cold sinks through her. She asks him to take his blazer off, to let her wear it. She is chilled to the bone, she tells him, dying of cold. He takes his wallet out the inside pocket, flips it open. Now, he'll show her his sweetheart, she thinks. But he takes out his own college ID and points to the picture: *I want you to see what I looked like when I was sober.* In the photograph, he is good-looking, slim-faced, jaw pressed proudly out. Now there is one large fold of fat in which his face is propped up. She takes his hand and places it on her lap. She doesn't mind. This is the easy stuff.

She was the one who taught herself to read. *B* and *A* makes *BA*. Everyone asked her, incredulous, *How did you do that?*

He lists back and falls off his stool, takes her with him. She is lying above him: flotation device, emergency raft. It takes a long time for the patrons to turn their heads, to witness the wreckage. She gets off him and pulls at his hand, but he is heavy, dead weight at the bottom of a slippery rope. *He's bleeding*, she says, and three big men come to hoist him up.

Such a pretty house, she says, despite herself. It's his parents' house. Large enough so he can lumber up the back stairs without waking them up, a house designed around its blind spots. She remembers a talk she attended when she was in her early twenties. The architecture of estrangement. She had liked the title, but the talk itself had been garbled, a series of simple words at the mercy of impossible sentences.

She doesn't know what she has in mind. One night, negotiated into two. She'll lie down, open up, the nib of a fountain pen split neatly apart. He has regained some strength. He looks over at her on the landing, has forgotten how he got here, who she is. He tells her she ought to go. But then, he lays his hand on her breast and says: *Fuck . . . well, fuck.*

In the room, there are two twin beds, which he insists on pushing together. *I'm a gentleman*, he informs her. *You had me fooled*, she says. She lies down, closes her eyes, falls into shallow sleep: She is in a wading pool, filling a red plastic cup with water and pouring it back out. Happy as a clam. She likes to watch the water moving with her, draining out over the lip of the plastic tub. *You taste so good*, he tells her, his mouth wet, a dog lapping water up from its bowl. Salt and sand and sea urchins, she thinks, and the vanilla crap she spritzed at the waistband of her undies. How did she know to do that? *B* and *A* is *BA*. Just like that. He crouches over her; she opens her mouth just wide enough to let him in. This is what he tastes like: dirty dog, pickled organs, ashtray, grout.

She wakes up, throat dry, head in her mouth. The two beds have slid slowly apart, the man crucified on one, she clammed inward on the other. The last thing she remembers is his slim dick prying open her mouth. She rolls onto her side: one leg down and then another. She is jelly, the room a spinning top. She finds her backpack, rummages through it, puts on her pants, a shirt that is clean enough. His wallet is on the ground; a ten and three ones. She leaves the ten and takes the ones, then takes the ten and leaves the ones. She could wait for him to wake up, big boy in his tiny bed. She could stroke his head, beg him for a few more nights. But *this* cannot be *that,* she thinks. She returns to the wallet, takes the university ID and slides it into her pocket. He should know better: there is no way back to the past.

It is early in the town. Earlier than she thought. The stores are shut, the air still cool from the night. The gulls sway and swerve. They land on the lips of garbage cans, tipping beaks into wide-open mouths. She would not say: *I am hungry*. She might say: *I feel like a trash can emptied out.*

She used to say to her husband, if she can still call him that: *Not feeling is a feeling too.* ■

Kaveh Akbar

How Prayer Works

Tucked away in our tiny bedroom so near
each other the edge of my prayer rug
covered the edge of his, my brother and I
prayed. We were 18 and 11 maybe, or 19
and 12. He was back from college where
he built his own computer and girls kissed
him on the mouth. I was barely anything,
just wanted to be left alone to read and
watch *The Simpsons*.

We prayed together as we had done
thousands of times, rushing ablutions
over the sink, laying our janamazes out
toward the window facing the elm which
one summer held an actual crow's nest
full of baby crows: fuzzy, black-beaked
fruit, they were miracles we did not think
to treasure.

My brother and I hurried through sloppy postures of praise, quiet as the light pooling around us. The room was so small our twin bed took up nearly all of it, and as my brother, tall and endless, moved to kneel, his foot caught the coiled brass doorstop, which issued forth a loud *brooong*. The noise crashed around the room like a long, wet bullet shredding through porcelain.

My brother bit back a smirk and I tried to stifle a snort but solemnity ignored our pleas – we erupted, laughter quaking out our faces into our bodies and through the floor. We were hopeless, laughing at our laughing, our glee an infinite rope fraying off in every direction.

It's not that we forgot God or the martyrs
or the Prophet's holy word – quite the
opposite, in fact; we were boys built to
love what was right in front of our faces:
my brother and I draped across each
other, laughing tears into our prayer rugs.

CUBA

Vanessa Onwuemezi

Policeman walks towards her, gun swinging from his hip, cracked stones rolling beneath his feet, head lifted high by some   vapours which only he can sense in cold blue air. Moves as if he's standing still and it's the earth that aids him, aids him forward.

His uniform is olive green, gun hovers by her open window, a hand on the roof and all is still, the birds hold their breath while she feels the engine vibrating through her seat.

'Buenos días, señora,' he says.

'That for cracking coconuts?' she says to the gun.

He laughs, then a gesture with the hand.

Now she stands, leaning against the car warms her thigh, grey smoke as the engine burns a veil to cloak her mouth and nose, while she flirts with tired eyes, body soaked in this morning's sweat, the dew, gathered as she passed through border after border on this long drive.

He looks at the exhaust, the smoke. 'Oil,' he says.

'Okay,' she says.

'Your name?' He leans himself against the car, clink of the gun.

'Cuba.' A lie.

True enough to her, grown up breathing the vapours of a place she's never been

Cuba   edging round the fields.

Cuba, rubbing its   legs together from the long grass.

Cuba, dripping warm from her eyelashes as she steps out of rain later that morning, into a hotel, in a coastline Spanish town.

The hotel is pink all over, as the bitten inside of her mouth, as her dark father's radiant bottom lip, as the scar stretching down the back of her mami's calf   then there's an oil lamp burning, a blackened ceiling, the baby's head wet with tears.

'The hotel was white,' says the receptionist, 'but it wanted to be pink.' He smiles, hands her the key card, 'Fifth floor.'

Behind him, another receptionist shuffles quiet feet, trying to catch a mosquito in a jar, 'Coño,' his mouth not so quiet, 'I don't like to kill.'

She loops her bag handles over her arm, slip   down to her elbow along hairs wet with rain. The arm aches under the weight.

Smoking on the terrace, she ignores the English man sitting easy with tall glass in hand, legs outstretched, like a grassy bank rolling into sand into a cold sea. The terrace is framed by hotel-room windows set into the flesh of the walls, meekly dressed in greyed netting. The terrace wants a pool or a fountain, something to draw the eye. Any noise echoes from the walls like the click-ripple of a stone into water.

His glass finds its way to her table, the sound of metal dragging over the tiles and he says cigarette? She doesn't answer, but looks up into his red-stained eyes and hands him the one in her mouth.

'Can't get enough of this   sunshine.' He inhales.

Her ear starts ringing and she's deafened on one side for a moment. Views his mouth slightly parted, dumbly. Cracked fingernails. Hair falls wiry around his ears and nearly to his shoulders, sips his beer, foam gathers to a drop of milk and hangs from his bottom lip. He's young, from the way he talks, but looking as if each year has doubled up on his face, his back hunched like stem of yellow flower drooping. He's been here a while, he says to her, looking out for himself, left the business he started under the care of a friend. He lies, she can taste it. He touches her arm too many times. The cigarette smoke reminds her of the car and the two dogs she saw hanging from a tree by the road.

Excuses, makes her excuses and leaves.

In her room, Mami is sitting on the edge of the bed holding an unlit cigarette, staring at the wall. She was never a smoker. 'When will you let me go?' she says. She's been moving things around. On the table in the corner, white plastic cups of water in a circle, Cuba walks over to look at her own warped face – eye, half-mouth, chin.

She scours online for a job and a new place to stay, 06/05 Agency staff required, and a number to call.

The Sixth of May calls her back that afternoon. And a day after that, she's handed a maid's uniform and a key card in a room beneath some stairs, open the door and in comes the frantic reflection of light from a swimming pool, chlorine and waft of blossom, while flies, not yet lazied by the stretch of summer, rush in and out again.

He had eyed her figure for her dress size, lingering over her stomach, down to her legs. She pulls at her shirt, tight over her belly. A ball of heat familiar burns down her throat, to work its way through her and lodge itself somewhere. Good. As long as it's somewhere hidden, it's all good.

'You're staying where?'

'Manolo Hotel, for now.'

'You're looking?'

'Sí.'

'There's a board.' He points at a large square on the wall across the room, above a worn sofa, paper notices.

She nods.

'Come from?'

'UK,' she says.

'Where else?'

'Y soy Cubana.'

He walks over to a locker and taps it with his middle finger, reaches inside his pocket, pulls out a padlock and keys which he throws in her direction. She holds out a hand and watches the metal crash onto floor tiles. A crescent echo lingers in the air, in an arc from his hand to the floor. She sees it. Just as she sometimes observes the moon separated out into image after image, tracking its movement across the sky   frame frame of the moon. At the same time, in her ear, the low croak of frogs mating at night.

'Be careful!' He steps into sunlight coming through the door. Two illumined grey hairs in his moustache. 'I won't give you another.' Sucks his teeth.

A knock at the door, weak as the crack of paper. A blonde woman stands in the doorway, dressed for work.

'Noda,' he introduces. At Noda's feet a fly crawls a centimetre along the floor   stops.

'You ready?' she says to Cuba, who nods.

Noda leads her up a floor and explains, mouth running quick Spanish, taps her finger on the coloured lids of plastic containers, spray bottles, cloths, towels, plastics, bedding, on a trolley outside of room 166. 'You're supposed to use this cloth for the dirty stuff, everywhere a normal person would put their ass. This one for everywhere else in the bathroom.'

Cuba's mouth searches for words in Spanish, hasn't spoken it in a long while, strains her mind forehead tightens, later, rubs her temples on the bus home.

In the room, she unmakes the bed while Noda watches, between opening the curtains, emptying bins.

'Not bad, but you'll have to speed up. You'll have all this floor and another to do. We cut corners.' She takes a sheet between two fingers and laughs, a bottomless laugh, while miming a scissor motion. She shows Cuba how to fold the corners beneath the mattress, pull it taut, tuck it under, pulls it all out and makes her start again, hair now in wisps around her neck as they hold between their fingers the quivering white.

A studio apartment, eighth floor, facing a wall on one side. The light dim it feels like she's half sunk into the ground. On the other side, in the distance she can see a square, the plaza. The kitchen is tidied away in a cubby with a small table, where she puts a little bottle of rum she found in a hotel room, and two chairs. 'Oye, tú qué haces aquí?' she hears Mami say, the voice mixing into the smell of plantain and beans, cucumbers long as cold running water, dusted with black pepper, and avocado felt up with a palm and five fingers for it to be hard and soft enough, to be ripe. Mami stands next to the kitchen table, pulling plates filled with food out of her shirt and dropping them heavy, she's angry, picks up a tea towel and curses, 'Cabrona, no te metas conmigo.' Whip-snaps it in the air.

Suitcase unpacked, Cuba stares out of the window towards the plaza, a stone stretched flat under the sun, light pushing away shadow to its edges. Mami stands nearby, calmer, the remembered smells still emanating from her. She's mouthing words as if in prayer, her lips feeling their way around a song from an old tale, isé kué, ariyénye, isé kué, ariyénye, isé kué, ariyénye, isé kué, ariyénye, droning as she watches people walk past down below, sloughing off the colours of their tanned feet and leaving it all to melt on the pavement slabs   brown, window cracked a little, wafting in the brown of skin.

With a square of burlap and purple cloth, Cuba tries to create from memory something she lost. Stones, shells, herbs, anise, all tied up with string. Mami had been a santera, priestess, a good one, had made her a charm tied with seven knots of string to ward off bad spirit. A charm, a desire, so slow to bend things, powerful and slow like water cutting through stone.

She folds and unfolds her bed sheets, getting better at smoothing out the creases with a slick hand. She knocks a breast and gasps, cups it, breast sore, full engorged, takes off her bra and squeezes.

D own in the plaza she lights a cigarette while her ass finds a chair and sits, winces at the heat of metal, a hot egg rolling under her thigh. She goes walking with the cigarette burning between her fingers, finds a museum, looks into a crypt from the top of the stairs, walls the red of clay, graves gaping open like a mouth of pulled teeth. Alone, she goes inside and waits a while in the cool, saying her own name out loud to the bones and clean smiling skulls.

Looping around to the port, she walks through drowsy streets with regular palm trees that droop towards her as she passes, shrubs bursting with pink blossom, lawns, behind them hills like dusty mounds, all a faded rush of grass with no beckoning. No promise.

A dog edges over and sits beside her while she's stopped to look, scratches its snout and follows in her shadow as she moves on, dipping its nose to the ground every once in a while like a shishi-odoshi, its eyes never meeting hers, never leaving her.

They pass the two policía, this time they're dressed navy, one policeman's eyes on the mongrel. He pulls his baton from the loop in his belt, pushes the dog with it, dog carries on after her. 'Perdón,' Policeman says, and shows her the underside of his hand.

He shoves the dog hard with his foot and it falls over, feet skitting across the brick with eyes rolling like oranges falling to the ground, or the roll of her father's fists when he was starting a fight, moustache a lump of charcoal crackling under his nose. 'It's Cuba, rotting his bones,' Mami used to say, but tapping her head. The dog stays on its side, gnashing its pale gums, drooping teats on its underside sunk into a cavern of ribs. Its outline dissolves in a moving network of fleas against sun-bleached brick of the pavement. Takes Cuba's focus away   brick brick   all the same, as she walks away.

As she moves, she feels her hips roll like her father's fighting fists, pumping her along until she reaches the port, stares at the yachts, tame sea.

As May turns to June to July she edges around the balconies of the hotel, room after room, encircling the large swimming pool, her arms darken as the sun empties its hot lungs into the months.

She swipes the card to room 160, enters and her arm hairs rise up. A dark room confronts her, and then on turns a hanging bulb lit electric bright straight ahead of her, dust idles around it before falling in to kiss the glass. Beneath it, where the dresser should be, is a small round table standing on a straw mat, on that a bowl of oranges, agua de florida, a miniature bottle of rum, seven seashells and a statuette of the Virgin in blue.

'Mami?' she says. It isn't Mami, the room is too cold, the absence of love. She takes off her clothes, she has to, something hot running between her legs, kneels in front of the altar and closes her eyes. She holds out a hand, trying to conjure nothing into something, into the courage of a beating heart, feels an orange squeeze down her throat pushing her lungs apart gulps and swallows, and then starts to cry and out of her mouth comes birdsong, the parakeet, the nightjar, the whistling duck, the flycatcher, the vireo, the cartacuba, the bullfinch, breaking into a wail like a dog to a coarse howling baby's cry.

Light breaks into the room, soft through her eyelids, Noda has opened the curtains, bustles around, quick vowels barely pausing for breath. She breaks wind and laughs, a brief pause in her cursing and scolding.

'Sixteen more rooms you've got on this floor. Mierda! How are you this slow? Why am I helping you? You're lucky you look like someone I knew once. Fuck you.' She hastily pulls the sheets from the bed piling them onto the floor. 'Why do I find you so often   staring at the wall like that?'

Cuba goes to wipe the tears from her eyes, but they're dry.

Noda, crossing the room. 'This is too much for anyone, sore hands, broken knees, my blood pressure, it's stress. They'll notice you getting slow, are you sick?' she says, 'Ten cuidado. Take it easy, but work hard, Cuba.'

She mentions a meeting, why she came up to find her. Her voice disappears in a din of plastic bottles hollow-knocking from the bathroom.

She emerges, 'Are you coming?'

'Yes.' Without knowing to what.

'I'll send a message.' Noda leaves, fast as she came, her rubber shoes squeaking a loose sole.

The tiny courtyard of the bar smells of ash. 'There's a movement starting in Barcelona, we should do the same.' Noda is near shouting. 'Thirty rooms a shift, these subcontractors are evil.' Her friend, who works in a hotel near the crypt, nods her head regular in time with music from the bar. A muted television screen high on the wall shows a forest on fire and a rising column of smoke, grey-yellow.

The day of the altar was a warning. Like Mami, the bad spirit had caught up with her, making itself known to her over and over, like the echoes of the objects in front of her eyes   spat out at regular points in space, a padlock, the moon, perpendicular to logic.

She sees the face of her baby in random encounters: a young boy in the street, a teenager she encountered in a corridor, young boys, baby boys encountered on the walk home   encountered   in the little boys running wet by the pool   skin a mass of drips of gold, in the faces she passes in the plaza in the cool hours, the child   encountered as the small brown bird shrieking at her from its perch in a tree, toenails lengthened to gripping claws. Child from the dark of her mind, intent on having her die of shame   ah   had her inflamed.

She feels the charm tight in a pocket, pulls at a coil in her hair and notices, from their table wedged in a corner, the manager from her first day, and another she's seen in the hotel, decorated with a gold name badge, name beginning with 'E', he wears polished shoes long and square, upturned at the tips like rowing boats. She taps Noda's arm and tells her the news, Noda freezes mid-sentence, turns and smiles them over, on the offensive. Manager, named Oko, has a little muscle pulsing beneath his eye, no smile but nods in her direction. 'E' introduces himself, speaks like his tongue is glued down, she doesn't catch the name. She tries a smile her lips sticky with vodka-lemonade. It gets busy. People edging sideways past tables, holding cigarettes   smoke   tracing the path of the summer's rising heat. A heavy feeling settles in her stomach. She forces out a cough.

There are more meetings like this. In bars, not so much – in apartments, back rooms of churches, loaned garages, the library, a word or two exchanged by lockers, an arrangement, a touch of the hand: we need sick pay, contracts, managers are nervous, the maids' faces give nothing away.

Noda comes by whenever their hours overlap, or comes to her home. She runs by Cuba every tentative word of an email, a bulletin, a speech for an audience day by day becoming   less imaginary. Barcelona on her lips, her mouth's oil, Lanzarote, Las Islas Canarias, Ibiza, sticky over her fingers, combed through her hair. Standing on her imagined podium, belly roll beneath her shirt, her back straight, and calloused hand curled into a fist. The same words are affirmed every time, sisterhood, solidarity, love, freedom, truth   bleed into the daily rhythm of the work: curtains pulled, sheets stretched flat over mattress, spray, brush, cloth on glass, on glass, day by day by day. Cuba's knuckles crack as she raises a pot from the stove, pours coffee for the two of them. 'Work and work and work, mija, until you're dead,' Mami used to say, and laugh.

And work, the work goes on, it does. Cuba edging around the balconies feeling like she's being watched. Oko edging around the balconies after her, ever nodding in her direction, nothing better to do.

A Thursday, she dusts each crease of the heavy curtains, smooths down the bedding, scrubs the toilet, shower, wipes a towel over the bathroom marble until it shines enough, goes to leave room 188 and Oko stands in the doorway, holding a finger-width rail of wood which he waves around in a figure of eight in front of her face, looping around her head until his moderate skill loses its nerve. Showing off   a threat? Should she be impressed? She makes a show of being impressed.

'Silambam,' he says at last, face and neck wearing a damp sheen, 'a martial art. Es de la India.' His shirt stretches tight across his belly as it throbs with quick breath, a glimpse of hair creeping close to the skin, black moss, curled like the dark hair on his head.

He continues to show up outside of the rooms she's working in. She has been keeping up the numbers, thirty rooms a shift, cutting corners, drinking up leftover wine, and swiping forgotten cigarettes, bottles of nail polish, alcohol, cologne and perfume. And he has never come with an accusation.

She's on the floor cleaning as he walks in, tapping the wall with that stick, then the floor, closer he moves. She's found a stain behind a dresser, no one has thought to look there, or had the time. Coffee, old stain has etched itself into the wall. She's been hypnotised by the rubbing, aching arms and shoulders but keeping it up, rubbing off the dark brown, releasing the wall's memories, the coffee – spilled or thrown – thin layers of paint, green, white beneath.

Oko taps her shoulder with the stick. Then, crouches to tap with a finger on her skirt at the crack of her ass. She doesn't turn around, yes her blood pressure is raised a little, and she has already decided that if he goes further she will submit. (Alone, rubbing her own breasts, swollen and ripe, and legs opening to welcome her fingers between the tops of her thighs. What she thinks about at times like this, when what is about to happen happens.)

He stands up and leaves, because of her silence, perhaps. Or the charm always grasped in her pocket. Or a noise in the corridor outside. She doesn't see him on shift again. Whenever a group of them gather, he gives up his seat for her.

Another meeting, it's evening. Women and some children enter the room, sombre as a low-hanging mist. A mass of heads

and clasped hands. They don't say much to each other, until
Noda begins.

> 'We don't have the right to get sick
> because   because
> they fire us
> immediately
> health and skin
> on the floors that we clean
> god of fury
> empower us.'

And people are on their feet, clapping hands together, fanning their
faces with folded paper, or waving it above their heads. 'Fair pay,
sisterhood, freedom,' chanted with the defiance of all the uprisings
begun in a small room, the fire in a drop of blood. The spirits, good
and bad, are present and alert. Cuba stands and cheers, soaking in
the power of the hands beating as tight-skin drums. 'Sin muerto
no hay santo', 'There's no Orisha without the spirits of the dead',
the words in her ear, she's soon doubled over with a pain in her
abdomen and a light head, having avoided water for the past few
days, avoiding the toilet because she's pissing blood. She takes
herself to the bathroom, quiet, but there are tiny flies fussing around
the room, excited by the cheering, riding on reverberations in the air
that will travel outwards indefinitely.

She sits in a cubicle and takes the charm from her pocket –
digging into her – and asks for protection, for the bad spirit at her
side to forgive. Ever since that day on the steps of the hospital,
when she had put down the bag and had started driving, there has
been a dense mass in her mind, in her stomach, working its way
through her. A seedless fruit lodged in her womb and rotting.
Bad spirit   an imbalance that permeates all things, like the smoke
from a bush fire thousands of miles away, where sky glows the
amber of flame, breaking in new days, new afternoons.

The toilet door opens. 'Cuba,' Noda says. The movements of her arm in flickering light as she bats away the flies.

'Sí, Noda.' From the cubicle. Gripping her belly.

'Estás bien?'

'Estoy enferma. Don't worry, go back in there.' A quick in-breath.

'Have you done a test?'

'No it's not that. Not that.'

'Oh honey, qué mierda.' Noda's hand appears in the gap beneath the door, flexing and wriggling her fingers in some kind of solidarity. Her face appears skin drooping to one side. She's a grown woman, Noda, Cuba finds the space to think of that. Slow tears reach her chin and drip into her hands.

Baby's cry had pealed out through the bag when she reached ten metres away. Her aching arm remembers the baby boy's soft weight, her ears, the cry that clung to her as she resisted any urge to look back.

'Cuba, don't worry,' Noda's disembodied head says from the floor. 'We'll take care of it. Sometimes bad things infect us. We'll sort it out, I'm telling you. Come on, Cuba, it's just one bad thing   that's all it is.' ■

Hourglass. Calcutta is an hourglass and each person is a grain of sand. Each day, we all pour through the opening. Every morning, each of us begins to slide downwards. By night all of us have squeezed through to pile up below. The trajectory of the day is different for each of all 15 million of us, but at the end point we find ourselves in extremely close proximity to everyone else. Of course, some of us don't make it to the other side. Every day several thousand grains just disintegrate in the crush and disappear, while many other thousands leak out, escaping the gravitational hug of the city to travel in different directions. As for the rest of us, we stay piled up on each other through the night, waiting for the morning to nudge us again and send us on our way.

It makes no sense at all, of course. The 15 million figure is for the sprawl of the Kolkata Metropolitan Area, aka Greater Calcutta, while the strictly defined area of the city is home to just four and a half million people. On a normal working day roughly another four million individuals commute into the hourglass and pour back out into the hinterland in the evening.

But, still, could it be that every individual's day in the city has a fulcrum? A narrowest point? And at what moment do you feel you've made it through to the other side?

Thinking of fulcrums brings me to thinking of weight. Between the hours of 6 a.m. and 11 p.m., the weight of human beings pressing down upon the area of the city proper doubles. Between evening and dawn the pressure disperses. The hourglass flips over, but remains in the same place. Why doesn't the ground give way under this repeated onslaught? Or does it?

RUCHIR JOSHI

Tremulously perched just north of one of the biggest deltas in the world, despite its 300-year-long pretensions to solidity and stability, Calcutta has a constant sense of something shifting underfoot. The ground underneath, according to some geological definitions, should not be called ground at all, made up as it is of layers of silt deposited over millennia by the River Ganga. Think of monumental blankets of mud entangled with each other, their shifting thicknesses embedded with massive pockets of water. Or imagine that below the top layer of earth the whole city is actually supported by an immense water table interrupted by sodden partitions of soil and rock. Then think of the buildings coming up and wells being sunk to pull out water. Imagine thousands of such buildings pulling up the water from underneath themselves, gallons and gallons of it every day, and then think of the man sitting on a high branch sawing the wood at a point between himself and the tree trunk.

Layers below, tectonic, horizontal. The vertical man-made things rising out of this earth also layered, as though they've sucked up the shifting and scraping below through roots of brick, cement and iron.

There are times of the day when it feels as though this – one of the most densely populated cities on the planet – is made up entirely of traces and residues, shredded palimpsests, ghosts of scaffolding all stacked on each other. A town of cards, a frontage-ville, a junkyard of abandoned movie sets where no picture can ever be finished, where even the screens and box offices are fading, painted backdrops.

Think of a constant background of thick tropical vegetation in front of which history plays mischievous optometrist, inserting and removing walls and buildings as though they were lenses.

Walking past walls in this city, I'm often reminded of one of my favourite painters, the American Jasper Johns, and his work from the 1950s and 60s. Most people here have never heard of Johns, and yet, somehow, everyone seems to have internalised his famous precept: Take something and do something to it. Then do something else to it.

Someone once told me: 'Calcutta is the bastard child of geography and colonial greed, and it has seen off every kind of capitalism there has been.' The opposite could also prove as true: new forms of capitalism will see off every kind of Calcutta there has ever been.

Sometimes it feels as though Calcutta has also seen off every kind of history there is. 'If you truly want to see the end of history, come and visit Calcutta.' But we know this can't be so – it's history that always does the seeing off.

Perhaps the weight of history is the collective weight of every person who has lived and died in this city over three centuries. A lot of history has been buried here, but, equally, a lot of it has been cremated daily.

This is a settlement fundamentally sculpted by water: floods, tides, indefatigable damp, river and rain – more kinds of rain than there are shades of green in the jungle. But woven through the genealogy of water, there's also one of fire, a long history of cooking fires on the street, small winter fires, blazes, conflagrations, riot bonfires and strategically executed arson.

Unlike in other towns, here the fire hazards are blind to class; you can find tinderboxes distributed everywhere: in slums and the old commercial buildings abutting the stock exchange, in nineteenth-century port warehouses and modern hospitals, in Edwardian piles and apartment towers with brand-new cladding.

We know better than most places how, whether through oil, electricity or perverse human agency, fire can piggyback on water.

The flyover came up about twenty-five years ago. It wasn't right next to the apartment where I live, but there was only one row of buildings between it and me. A gap between buildings allowed me to see a sliver of it, the traffic noise funnelling through to my fourth-floor window. The honking from the big avenue below was now amplified by the overhang – a whole new road had been added on top of an already overcrowded one.

Now, the first night sounds come after 11 p.m., when the supply trucks are released from the municipal borders and allowed to enter the city. The road below the flyover is a major artery and the truck horns doppler past my balcony till the early hours of the morning. The flyover is one of the few clear stretches of road in the city without bumps or traffic lights, making it great for drag racing. At some point after midnight the rich boys start with their fancy, heavy motorbikes, hammering by in ones and twos, east to west, west to east, till it's time to pay off the traffic cops and go home. There is an interval, a feint of silence, before the street dogs launch into their nightly opera, the glissandos of howling and percussive barks bouncing off the buildings. After the dogs comes the sound of small hooves drumming on the asphalt, a march of goats, interrupted by stick taps and clicking sounds from the mouths of the men herding them to the meat shops. A small truck passes by, the open back packed with labourers heading somewhere. Inching towards dawn, someone in the next building switches on the water pump to fill their tanks. The pipe outside my bedroom window starts to shake and clank; I know it's neither burglar nor water, just the two mongoose-like creatures heading down from their nightly hunt to go hide in the small clump of trees at the juncture of three building compounds. A faint prickle of noise turns from mechanical to melodic – the first azan from the mosques a mile away. As the dawn begins to firm up, there is birdsong from the trees. By 7 a.m. all other sounds are hammered down under the rumble and scream of the day's traffic.

Growth climbs onto growth. A tropical forest is made up of many competing things; there's a continuous argument between different kinds of vegetation about what belongs and what doesn't. A city built on a swamp can easily take on the characteristics of what it has tried to tamp down.

People often speak of time as a running river. Here time becomes a swamp, the days and weeks bubbling and turning in solipsistic swirls. It often feels as though the city has no present and no future, as if the only thing growing here is the past, the misremembered twining around the half-remembered in an ever-thickening jungle of memories.

Every day the city seems to sink a bit under the load of this ever-present past. But then you realise: it's not that the city has no present or future, it's just that the present and likely futures are different from those available to other cities. It's just that history does its sums differently here and comes up with strange answers.

At certain points history strikes a match and situations are gutted by fire. At other times structures collapse under the weight of their contradictions.

March, 2016. In north Calcutta a section of a flyover under construction came crashing down at midday. Several people died. I went there two days after the event with my friend SC who is a press photographer. The immediate clearing up had finished, the easily reachable bodies taken away, the injured shifted to hospital. Right at the crossing of two roads, the fallen slabs made a kind of high awning, under which different emergency crews and salvage workers were carefully shifting the debris while sniffer dogs nosed around for bodies under the rubble.

SC and I decided to get to a rooftop. The building we went into was built in the early twentieth century as a sort of middle-class tenement for traders from western India. The entrance led to a courtyard lit by a stained-glass skylight five floors above. The blue light falling on the chessboard of the marble floor briefly pulled us into a different world. We took the wooden stairway and came out onto the terrace that overlooked the collapsed slabs. The area has some of the oldest surviving buildings in the city, many of them sealed off for being hazardous but impossible to demolish because of protracted property disputes. Around us we could see the maze of tilted, almost toppling brick and woodwork and ramshackle masonry that visiting photographers love to shoot as typical of Calcutta.

Leading away eastward from the crossing was the completed portion of this flyover which was supposed to connect the airport and the railway station at two different ends of the city. From here it looked as though a dirty grey river of concrete had rammed its way through the architecture, the asphalt flooding everything up to the second floor of the roadside buildings. At places the edge of the roadway was literally inches from the windows and balconies of the old houses. I knew of nowhere else in the world where someone would conceive of such public engineering, much less actually try and execute its construction.

The 'accident' below us was also part of this kind of engineering, resulting from a cat's cradle of corruption that criss-crosses from the current state government to the previous regime to the construction companies and the Public Works Department officials charged with overseeing them. From above, the broken structure managed to pull off a strange trick: on the one hand it looked as if it had been dropped the previous night by aliens, and yet – this being Calcutta – it also looked perfectly woven into the surroundings, as though it had been there, in exactly this state, for decades.

'Nothing new can ever be added to this city. It has to be already old, flawed or damaged for the city to accept it.' I can't recall who said this to me, but I remember thinking about it while looking down at the crashed concrete.

RUCHIR JOSHI

We used to be world champions, once: the poorest city in the world, the most populous city in India, the most overcrowded place in the 'Third World', the worst urban agglomeration on the planet. We had the highest disease rates, the worst sanitation, the largest number of infant deaths. For a good thirty years between 1960 and 1990, we were *the* end-of-the-world destination, the anti-New York, the anti-London, the anti-Tokyo, the city which was the polar opposite of the great cities of the world where money was made, where people thrived, where things worked. There was actual Calcutta, with its real miseries and tragedies, and there was the Calcutta of international imagination, the worst urban hell you could visit on the planet.

Sometime during the 1960s, photographing Calcutta became an international safari sport. Western photographers began to visit, either directly or stopping by on their way to or back from Vietnam (Look! Human devastation can happen even without the help of napalm!), shot rolls and rolls of film and carried back their emulsion trophies to print on the pages of magazines or hang on their walls.

Rapidly a currency developed of Calcutta pictures, an immediately decipherable image vernacular to compete with famines in Africa and exotic rituals from Bali. The 'icons' from Calcutta that became established were 'starving child', 'begging mother and child', 'rickshaw puller in the rain', 'protest procession by communists', 'the heroic nun ministering to the dying'. This was leavened by 'positive' images of the Durga Puja, when the Mother Goddess is celebrated and the clay statues slide into the grey-green river.

The old titles have been removed now, taken away from us. Cities in other countries are far more terrifyingly disastrous; Calcutta now has fewer people than Delhi or Bombay, though we're still the most tightly packed. The one thing that still adheres to the city is the husk, the simulacrum, of a once-great culture. And yes, despite not having any industry like Bombay or anywhere near the number of motor vehicles Delhi has, we are still the ones with the worst air, water and sound pollution among major Indian cities.

RUCHIR JOSHI

For most of last year, during the various degrees of pandemic-induced lockdown, I stayed at home in my flat. When I'd returned from a trip in December 2019 I had no idea that I would be spending more than 400 days straight in this city. With the arrival of the virus, the hourglass of the city stopped flipping over quite so regularly. Things changed.

Within a few days the air was no longer recognisable, as though someone had done a transfusion, siphoning away the old atmosphere and replacing it with a new clean one. The curfew brought with it smells sharpened by the absence of pollution: tea boiling on a coal fire on the street two buildings away, asafoetida being ground in an unseen kitchen nearby, onions frying in another house, pungent garbage sorted by the scavenging crew next to the expensive cars in the building parking lot next door, trees releasing scents.

Suddenly the wall of traffic noise disappeared, as if someone had kidnapped all the cars and buses. The springtime birdsong from the clump of trees outside my building exploded into a variety I'd never heard before. Had so many different birds been there every spring, inaudible under the cacophony? Or were there more kinds now, because of the air? I could smell and hear new things but the view from my windows remained the same. Had the city been replaced by a completely different one just beyond my sight lines?

When politicians used to say they wanted to transform Calcutta into the 'Singapore of India' you had to burst out laughing. But then people like me would fall into the trap of imagining a futuristic city as radically different from Singapore or Shanghai as possible.

Just as the pandemic whisked away the future for resculpting, it also removed these fantasies of mine. Walking the streets again after the Covid-19 lockdowns, it suddenly struck me: the mistake, when thinking about Calcutta's future, is to imagine 'improvements' or 'better amenities', or 'amazingly innovative green architecture' or 'a more equitable city'. To put it differently – it's not that Calcutta has no future, it's that Calcutta has leapfrogged over the present of most cities and reached the future ahead of them.

Sometime in the mid-1980s I interviewed a French genetic scientist who was visiting Calcutta for a study. He told me: 'People in Calcutta would be much better equipped to deal with a post-nuclear holocaust than those in almost any other city in the world.' It took me a moment to understand that he meant Calcutta was already approaching the conditions that would follow a thermonuclear exchange.

Perhaps in our minds nuclear war was a simpler thing then, a single cataclysmic event leading shortly to the end of the world. Now we can see other horrible possibilities, simultaneous apocalypses which leave us not wiped out but in an elongated inferno, with the cremation grounds shifting from riverbank to parking lot to the sides of the highways.

Given our interminable relationship with calamity, I can't help thinking that Calcutta is still better equipped than other places to deal with this not-quite-end of history.

History began to shift the weight of the city in 1942, when the first wave of refugees started to arrive – Bengalis who had trekked home from Burma, which had fallen to the Japanese army. The next wave was much bigger, the gravity of hunger sucking in several hundred thousand peasants from Bengal's villages, ravaged by the war-made, administration-authored famine; many thousands died on the pavements, many thousands survived and stayed. The next influx came during Partition, with Hindus leaving the two thirds of Bengal that had become East Pakistan, followed by another wave in the early 1950s. The last big addition to the city's population was in 1971, when several million people crossed the border to escape the genocide by the Pakistani army. Most of the refugees went back after the formation of Bangladesh, but many thousands stayed. Over the last eighty years Calcutta has multiplied in size and population and become a city of mutating scarcities and absences, a living museum of the temporary and unstable.

Here, a makeshift structure may remain installed for years, growing roots and branches. A street or a lane will stay unchanged over decades and then suddenly, for no apparent reason, chunks of it will disappear in the space of months, the crumbling old nineteenth-century brick walls embedded among blocks of concrete, sheets of glass and synthetic cladding, which in turn will rapidly take on the patina of decay.

Is history just a bad paint job on endless repeat? Or maybe more like an ongoing project of shoddy wiring. Recent layers peel off in the rain or steaming heat and marks emerge, marks you imagined were erased long ago. Some bad soldering and suturing from decades earlier send a current off course, causing short circuits and fatal fires in the overloaded network of the present.

Infinity, the prisoner on trial, is removed from the courtroom of the museum and disappeared. Erasure dances upon erasure. Take something away, take something else away. Something that should be there is never put in place, changing the balance of lives, shifting the fulcrum of a day.

Sometimes there is a short circuit of dodgy cement. Or large slabs of history drop suddenly, crushing a person as if they were a grain of puffed rice. ■

RUCHIR JOSHI

THE REPEAT ROOM

Jesse Ball

There was a long counter in the diner. The lights were on, but there wasn't much. It was light for someplace smaller than that, maybe the light from the dash of an old car. It would have to do. It was a small diner, really just the counter, and the counter was empty but for a man and a woman. The man sat and before him was a grayish envelope. He was not fifty, but not forty either. His arms and shoulders were solid. His hands looked abused, broken. His hair was badly cut, and his chalk eyes looked where he pointed them. Right then he was looking at the counter, at the envelope, not at the woman in front of him. She was just finished saying something.

She was somewhere between twenty and forty, with a face and body like a photograph of a waitress. On her neck in serif it said, CARLOS. Maybe it said, FOREVER, too. Her weight was on one foot or the other. What she said then was,

'Not that you should listen to me. I don't care. Just as a courtesy I'm telling you. That bell goes off means you got to be over there. People who take their time, they probably wish they hadn't. I've worked here a while. Take it for what it's worth.'

The man looked over his shoulder out the window. The building opposite had a massive entranceway funneling down to a tiny single bronze door. Beside it was a guard booth. The building was a courthouse. It was an edifice of stone, something like a pyramid. In monumental letters was written: COURT 5. Someone was walking up the steps, infinitely small in that place, scarcely human.

'They ask you to come down, I guess they can wait their turn too,' he said. 'And anyway, it's not like you've been inside there.' His voice was low and raspy. 'Maybe it's a picnic.'

'Suit yourself. What'll you have?'

He pointed to a menu inset in the counter. The waitress turned, went to a window in the wall and shouted through it,

'Number six.'

She pressed a button in the wall and coffee came out of a spigot into a cup she was holding. The next part of her dance was she put it in front of him and she looked at him and she looked through him.

'Service.'

The man could see through the window to the kitchen. A face had appeared there, a ruddy-looking cook, fat and dirty, a short-order cook. He put a plate on the partition and turned away. The cook and the kitchen flickered for a second and there was just wall there with a slot. Then it was there again and the cloth of the cook's linen-clad back was moving out of frame.

The waitress nodded to her customer.

'I used to ask people who they see in the hologram. For me it's my mom. No kidding. Twenty years dead but there she is. People say it's a man, it's a woman, one guy saw his brother. You remember when they put these in? People couldn't believe their luck. Now it's just garbage looking at garbage.'

'Must get lonely in here,' said the man. 'No one to talk to.'

'That's right,' she said, and gave him his plate.

Her hands played with the waitress pad, turning it over and over. It wasn't even paper. It was just a block looked like a waitress pad. You could see from her fingers she'd had a hard time. Fingers like that.

She was talking, mostly to herself, but she'd look up from time to time, like a child checking to see if it was asleep yet.

'I never envy the bastards who get the call. Pardon me, you're one of them, but it's the truth. I hope to God I never get that envelope in the mail. Me, I'm known to screw up anything and if I had to be a juror, well, I'd never make the cut. I mean if you knew you got to see it, got to see the room, well maybe it's worth it. Everyone's curious about the repeat room. But there's no guarantee. I mean it's the opposite. And that's the thing, huh. Mess up in there, end up ranked down. There you were doing nothing, just trying to get by. Never knew you looked so much like a rat, did you?'

The man did something like a smile.

'I mean, I'm curious,' she said. 'Surely I am. I want to look inside somebody's head. But I'd be afraid too. I've heard people die doing it, time to time. You heard that?'

He put some money on the counter, picked up the envelope, inclined his head and went out the door.

'You look like a nice type,' she called after him. 'Don't let 'em turn you around.'

The man stood in a room. He was in a line. Others were behind him. He had been at the end of it, but now he had come to the front. The paint of the walls was itself the room's light source and it was too bright for human eyes. The man squinted his and looked up at the glass. A woman was looking down. The space between them was a barrier, but there were metal slats. Whether he was hearing her or hearing her voice reproduced no one could tell. Still she spoke and he heard. She was wearing some kind of cloth helmet that covered her hair.

'State your name, occupation, age, place of birth.'

'Abel Cotter. Heavy-machine operator. Forty-six. Born Seaport District.'

'Put your hand in the box.'

A metal flap flipped up. It was somewhere he could put his hand. He did.

Something locked over his hand; it was stuck.

'Don't struggle. Just wait.'

A clicking noise came through the intercom.

'Not really a heavy-machine operator are you,' said the woman. 'More of a garbage man. Says here you're a garbage man.'

The people in line behind him shifted uneasily.

'It's a machine,' he said, head down.

'Around here we want the truth. You can go to the next room. Show 'em your number.'

As she spoke, a noise of hydraulics releasing came out of the hole and with it his hand. He rubbed at it. There were black symbols there like numerals. A door opened in the wall.

He went through it, and the person behind him took his place.

A lamp flickered on and off in the ceiling. Abel sat on a long bench. Ten or twenty people were beside him. The same opposite, just a few feet away. A girl with short hair wearing a tight sweater and not much else. Another girl wearing a cast on her arm. The man beside him stank of liquor, old liquor. A woman with dark glasses and a birthmark elbowed him as she sat. There really wasn't any space. It was like people say: a submarine, being on a submarine. Like that. Someone in the line was talking to somebody else, saying,

'They want you to get used to each other.'

'I don't think that's it.'

'Yeah, they want you to get used to each other. It's a competition.'

'It's not a competition.'

'But you can sure fuck it up.'

'Nobody knows that.'

Abel went with others into a room with lockers. There they changed out of their clothes and into other clothing, light-yellow colored robes, like hospital gowns, but more substantial. Some of the bodies he looked at in the room were soft and useless, others muscular. Some were male, some female. Everyone had to change in front of everyone else. The place was so squat and pitiless, so endless, repetitive, fluorescent. There was nothing sexual to be found there.

'Did you know it would be like this?' an old woman asked the girl next to her.

The girl was naked, trying to put on the uni-robe. She looked like a recruit. She wasn't bothered by anyone's eyes.

'It's not something to know,' she said. 'You just put your robe on.'

The old woman asked if anybody knew how long it was going to take. Someone told her to shut her mouth, shithead. Someone else told them, shut your mouth. Nobody was listening to anybody else, not really. The ceiling of the locker room was low. None of the lockers had locks, but there were cameras on the walls.

'You put your clothes somewhere. You come back later and get them. It's easy.' That's what the recruit told the old shithead.

Abel leaned against the wall a minute and closed his eyes. People were standing there near him, but he was inconsequential to himself, empty.

'The cool type, huh? Waiting it out? I get it. Don't worry, I get it. Probably the best bet.'

A short, low-slung man was crouched on his heels. Boyish and somehow prematurely old. His yellow garment touched the ground like a woman's dress. He wiped his nose roughly, like he was helping someone else do it. He winked at Abel.

A bell rang. Silence. It rang again.

'I guess that's the signal. We keep going deeper. Aren't you curious?'

Abel met the man's eyes. What was there was just spilloff.

They went down a hallway, in line like children, some stumbling here and there, unused to such order. The walls were nondescript. There was no signage. The floor was an oddly soft plastic, green like putty. The foot didn't sink into it, but the tromping of feet made no report. After ten minutes they came to a door, which the official unlocked. They'd watched her walk the whole way but she'd shown nothing, given no details. The task was to walk them in the hallway. When she was doing it, she was the one walking them in the hallway. There wasn't anything else there. This was the new way for people to be, the new era. The balsa wood can be used once, then it breaks.

'Find a place wherever you can.'

Room A was enormous and it was full of people dressed like they were dressed, like mental patients, lounging like full-time losers on the hard benches. The newcomers were no different, except they hadn't found seats. They were later than the others who must have come on time, or early, or even arrived here in the days before. It was a real gathering. No one was missing. Every sort of person was there. It had the cheap expectation of a carnival tent. Abel looked for somewhere to sit and saw it on the far side. He went there. A man with a cane was taking up two or three spots. Abel made him take up two, and sat in his own space, quietly, looking down at the marks on his hand.

The old man looked at him from time to time. He had thick white hair and heavy glasses under which his face shook without warning. He would take his glasses off and then put them back on again, God knows why.

'Do you think it'll be long?'

'I don't know.'

'Who is going to speak to us?'

Avoiding the question, Abel looked at his robe. Then he looked at the robes the others were wearing. Each of the robes had a number on it.

'Be careful,' the old man told him. 'Whole thing's a trick to get you to confess to something. Or to get you to do something you shouldn't.'

'Pshaw,' said a stocky woman on the other side. 'The only ones getting it are the ones who've got it coming.' Her hands were kneading her knees and her knees stuck out. The skin there was fibrous and peeling.

The old man inclined his head in disagreement.

A flat tone, unpleasant by design, loudened and filled the space until all speech ceased. A projection appeared on the wall and people turned to face it. The visage there was another official, not particularly male or female, but the voice was deep.

'This is the jury. You have been selected at random in order to be what you are now, a jury. The next three days, today, tomorrow and the next day are the jury selection, training and trial, a selection from the pool of candidates, from the group here assembled. As you perhaps have heard we will train you and in training you we will winnow you down until there is only one left. Everyone else will be removed, having demonstrated their unfitness. Only one person will be left, one fit person. That person will be the jury for the case in question. It will be this single opinion that makes the statement of life or death. You may be a coward. This has been taken into account. Do not try to evade the duty for which you are a candidate. The consequences for such behavior, such cowardly behavior, are severe. From now on all errors, misbehaviors, back talk, will be penalized under code 4429-762. This is not your regular life. Have a care.'

The projection blinked out, leaving just the warning behind.

A moment later the tone again. Then another projection.

What they saw was a jail cell and in it a man sitting on a stool. He looked up at the camera and said nothing. He was young, possibly still a teenager. He was several days unshaven and his eyes were ringed with sleep. In the cell you couldn't see how large he was. He could have been any size.

'This is the person for whom you are here. From time to time we will show you his image to acquaint you with your task.

'What do you think he did?'

The old man was right by his elbow.

'What do you think?'

'I don't know.'

'Must have been something bad.'

The old man laughed.

'Must have been pretty bad to get the death sentence, eh? Still I'd like to know. Kid like that, looks like a fuck-off. Dirty like that, like he was.'

'Looks like they make him sit in that cell, maybe it's not his fault he's dirty.'

'Oh, he's dirty all right,' said the stocky woman. 'I know hundreds just like him. That's the kind of neighborhood I live in.'

'It's not supposed to matter what he did, is it? That's not the job,' said Abel.

'That's right,' said the old man, 'not supposed to, but it does matter. It matters, doesn't it?'

'That's the point,' said Abel slowly. 'That's the whole thing. It's about what you'll do, not what you did.'

'Don't bother talking to him,' the woman told Abel. 'He's irrelevant.'

'I don't have to put up with this,' said the old man, standing up.

There was no place for him to go, though, so all he could do was sit down again.

'See, like I said. Irrelevant. Your time is done.'

The woman coughed into her hand. It sounded like part of her lung had come loose, but no one looked at her.

Now they sat at partitioned desks facing blocky screens like concave lamps. Abel wore thick headphones and stared into the centermost point where the light converged. Stare at the monitor. Stare at the monitor. Stare at the monitor. Be ready and speak. A small green sphere appeared. He said that. A flame like a candle but no candle. He said that. Something bony, an ankle, but without a foot or leg. A moment passed. It flickered away. A swishing tail, a cat's tail appeared, followed by a trombone, a contour map, a plate of spaghetti, a face biting its lip. He said what these were, rapidly, quietly. There was a meter on the wall of the partition. When he would answer quickly it would rise. When he would slow down it would fall. He sped up. Sock puppet. Battery pack. Musical instrument, no, dulcimer. Cartoon mouse. Teacup. Rose bush. Helicopter. The meter flashed at the top. Now someone was behind him, an official, helping him to his feet. He removed the headphones and followed the man out of the room, past dozens of desks. The muttering was loud taken together. Names of things without urgency said urgently, pulped into incoherence against what else was said, where the else was just what happened to be said. It wasn't even clear what you were supposed to say. They were all just saying what they saw.

The attendant walked ahead of him with a swaying step. Her shirt and pants were carefully fitted, but institutional. Her hair was in many small braids. She had the fragility of youth, but her face was serious, like someone who had been told a secret. The attendant took him down three or four hallways to a door marked EXAMINATIONS.

'I'm Marna,' she said. 'Sometimes I'll be dealing with your case.'

'Abel.'

'No, no, no,' she laughed.

She reached out and touched the number on his arm. 'This is who you are for our purposes. No names, please.'

She depressed a metal square on the wall. The door opened. Inside, three officials were sitting opposite a single chair.

'Please sit.'

The room was faced on one side with a mirror. Abel watched himself, watched the broken-down man sit in a plastic chair like he was told to.

'Why do you think this is the way it's done?'

He said he didn't know.

'Okay, smart guy. Then what do you think it is? What is the way it's done?'

He said so far it didn't make sense.

'What have you been told about it? What have you heard?'

He said he knew it was like a movie. Like you watched a movie, but it was a person who didn't know they were acting. They were having their real life to them.

'It is a person who doesn't know they are acting. They are in a special chamber, the room. This repeat room can be made to expose them to whatever experience we like. What they bring is themselves and how they are. We are judging that, we as a society. The juror is the agent of that judgment, the judger, the judge. A scenario is chosen, matched to what we know of them and what they've done. You may have heard of some of the scenarios. Have you heard of them?'

He said he had heard of one or two. There was one with a lost cat.

'The lost cat scenario. That one has seized the public imagination.'

A different official interjected,

'It's amusing, because it's so rarely seen, but it's the one that . . .'

'Yes, it's the one people think of.'

'Do you remember what it was like before? You were educated thirty to forty years ago. You were taught about the primitive court system. Are you in favor of that system? Many people your age think they are. They think that because they haven't thought about it. Are you?'

He said people can do what they like. His opinion so far hasn't mattered.

'But if it did?'

He looked at the officials for the first time. One was a red-headed man whose face beneath the eyes was covered with a thick beard like straw. The next was a girl, or practically so. She couldn't have been more than eighteen years old. Still it had been her doing the talking. The third was a bald man with a scar on his lip, something surgical or a knife injury. His eyes were very large and seemed kind. Where the others were upright he was bent, inclining as if in offering. He was farthest away.

'Well the other way didn't work so well,' said Abel cautiously.

The official laughed.

'Do you understand the difference between the systems?'

Abel inspected his feet. His toenails needed cutting, just like every other time he'd looked at them.

'It's useless,' said the bearded man. 'Look at his dossier. He's not suited.'

'Candidate,' said the girl. 'State the difference if you understand it between the two systems.'

'One punishes. The other looks forward.'

'So you've seen the billboards,' she said wryly. 'You don't always just look at your feet.'

He sat in a room by himself. It was a large room with many chairs. After a while someone came in and sat down. He didn't look at them. They didn't look at him. Another came. Then another. More came, none looking at the others. Soon there were many there, none of whom could say who they were near. None of them wanted to look and none did. They were all looking at the air a foot in front of their face. Not past that. When the seats were all full, the lights came up in the front. As one, the audience shifted and became still.

A man with a face like an old debt came out under the lights. He looked like he was about to speak. A woman followed him out, tapped him on the shoulder, whispered something. They argued briefly. He left the stage. The woman bowed and began.

'That was just a mix-up,' she said. 'That's the kind of thing happens when two people try to be in the same place at the same time. Kind of the problem we got here, only it's a thousand people trying to fit into one pair of pants. Not like you came of your own free will. Good citizens.'

She shook her head.

'Anyway, you got me here now, so let's start.'

Once she started talking, her voice was very loud, louder than anyone would expect. When she turned away and turned back, you felt it, even at a distance. Where she stood the ceiling was low. It was like she was standing in a box. There was something theatrical about it, the way the space outlined her. She seemed perfectly suited to it. The cuff of one of her sleeves was rolled up, but it revealed nothing. She was describing the execution process. Her mode of speaking was expansive.

'Jurisprudence should not have to do with the past. It is, like education, a promise of a future, a kind of future. The future is what?'

She gazed into the audience.

'It is what we bring to it together. Therefore the question posed is: who are we? Who gets to be a part of this group, we? Therefore the penalty of failing to appear fit is to be removed from the group. That is why the penalty is execution. It is not a matter of good and evil. It is a practical matter. When the cat scratches your sofa, you must question whether it is the right cat for you. Wrong cats do not stay in the house for long.'

She walked up the aisle and stood at the back of the audience. The heads did not follow her. They stared straight on, waiting for her to continue.

'I am an explainer. You are know-nothings. Ask me things and I'll explain them. Are there any questions?'

'How is it done?'

'How is it done.'

She repeated the question so everyone could hear it, but without emphasis, and walked back to the front of the room.

'Do you know ways it used to be done? Say them.'

People began to speak up like it was a classroom. Not knowing how they could please anyone, they showed their infallible immaturity and leapt at the chance to distinguish themselves.

'Drowning.'

'Hanging.'

'Electrocution.'

'Injection.'

'Guillotine.'

'Axe.'

'Shooting squad.'

'Made to walk in the desert.'

'They'd push you from a cliff.'

'Cut your throat.'

'Starve you.'

She nodded at each entry, listening carefully.

When she'd heard enough she raised one hand:

'Some of these are messy. Others simply work badly, inefficiently. People don't die the way they should, and it has to be done again. Generally, we find, executions were handled better long ago. The more people think people have value, the worse they are at killing them. This is true of course only in this case. In war we go on year by year, better and better at it. Yes?'

A woman with a shaved head and glasses had her hand raised.

'Which one is used now?'

'Isn't it interesting that no one here knows? For some reason, you aren't told that, the public. But you will be told now, for the reason that you should imagine it happening to the man you saw earlier today. You should imagine that in order to know what it is to take your job seriously. Does this make sense?'

Some heads nodded. Others stayed curiously poised.

'Let's look at him now. Let's take a look at him again.'

A projection blinked on behind her. The young man in the prison cell was there in the room with them. It was like he could see them there. He stood up and moved toward them, but there was only a few feet he could go. One of his eyes was a little red, and the second-to-last button on his shirt hadn't been fastened. There was an air about him – like a person at a food stall; somehow all of who he was hadn't been poured into his container. It was a person there, for sure, but visibly shallow. Yet his eyes were large in the room and to look that way was to look at them. He turned his thin back and the image winked out.

'The method is that the surplus person is put in a concrete room with a sealed door. After a little while the breathable air is removed from the room. Then biological death occurs. This process has no flaws and does not suffer from any of the difficulties of the old processes. It works one hundred percent of the time and costs the taxpayer almost nothing. Try all they like, the lungs learn they have no job to do.'

She made a little bow.

'The new society is not pretty. It just does what it can to not be false and to permit no falseness. Can you picture it? Can you try? Picture that boy in a concrete room, a kind of killing jar, yes? Feel your lungs now. Put your hands on your chest, please. Do that now.'

Everyone put their hands on their chest.

'Feel your lungs and how they rise and fall. Now hold your breath. Hold it as long as you can. Hold it until you can hold it no longer and your eyes swim in points of light. This is how you will kill him, if you choose to.'

'Next question,' the woman called. 'Don't be shy. It's not like we're watching your every move, waiting for a mistake . . .'

She laughed in spite of herself at that.

From behind Abel, a feeble voice said something. People turned. 'Say it again.'

Someone else spoke up, one person doing someone else a favor like you sometimes hear of.

'She said, is it dangerous?'

'Is what dangerous?'

The feeble one told the other one what was dangerous and the other one asked, 'They say jurors die with that helmet on. Is it so?'

The woman at the front bit her lip a little and scratched her face with one finger.

'The question, so everyone can hear it, is: do jurors die? The question was asked with regard to some of the equipment used in the process, that being a helmet that the juror wears when viewing the contents of the repeat room. Evidently some of you know more than others about this. We'll try to get you all onto the same page, as it were. I will answer this question now.'

She pulled a stool out and sat.

'The repeat room is a phenomenon, a process, that has been in use for ten years. Ten years. It's a long time. At the outset, its use was not perfected as it is now. There were cases at first where jurors were not capable of bearing the stresses of the task. There were deaths. But over the years there have been developments, and you need not fear for your safety.'

There were a bunch of questions then. People wanting to know what the developments were.

'Okay, all right, quiet now. One was pharmaceutical. There are medicines that blunt the ill effects. Another was behavior modification. You have some, let's call them, interactions, and the interactions put you in a frame of mind that's helpful. Finally, we have gotten better at finding people who can bear the stress, and also at identifying those who cannot. In any case, it is a part of life in this civil society, and no one has to do it twice.'

'When was the last death?' a man in the front row asked.

'There have been no deaths since the second year of institution. There really is nothing to fear anymore.'

'But what about sickness?'

'What if we're allergic to the medicine?'

'What if we decide we can't do it, just can't? Not me, I mean, but, just someone?'

'Where is the prisoner now? Is he in this building behind one of these doors?'

The woman held her hand up for silence.

'I think we may have gone through enough questions for now. Those of you who are here tomorrow will have the opportunity to ask more. For now let me leave you with this thought: if someone's life is at issue, isn't it a grave enough thing for a juror to take a risk herself to see if that life can be saved?'

Behind Abel, someone muttered,

'You don't save lives here, you take 'em . . .'

The speaker went to the door and opened it.

'I used to joke that if you were a good enough bunch, you wouldn't have to go right now to be cleaned, but, people didn't like the joke. Reason is, you're going to have to be cleaned no matter what you do. Into the hallway, please, one at a time.'

The same attendant, Marna, took Abel Cotter and the others to a hallway lined on both sides with shallow closets. On the glass partition it read again and again frontways and backwards H Y G I E N E . E N E I G Y H . H Y G I E N E . E N E I G Y H . All the way down.

Over the loudspeaker, a message came.

'Mandatory cleaning. Remove your garment and step inside.'

Abel looked at the closet, shook his head almost unconsciously, and looked back at the attendant. She pointed to the closet.

'I'm sorry. You have to comply. Remove your garment and step inside.'

The closet was narrow and the door was pretty heavy. It wasn't somewhere anyone wanted to go. He hung his garment on a peg, took a breath, got in and the door shut. He opened his mouth as if to scream, but no noise came out. Immediately it started getting hotter. It became hotter and hotter, hotter and hotter and hotter and hotter. Sweat formed on his back and chest and forehead, and he shook a little, like a worried animal. It felt like a trick. The door was an inch from his face. A horrific deep-frequency tone began, a tone so low he could hardly hear it. It shook his legs and chest. It shook his bowels. The noise grew worse and worse. It was all he could do to stand, and as he stood, he shat and pissed on his legs and feet. Almost immediately, as if in answer, the temperature began to decrease. Water sprayed over him from every direction. It was cold, very cold, then it became hot again, hotter and hotter. Finally there was just a mist that turned to nothing, then dryness. The dryness increased until he could feel his skin like paper. The door to the outside opened and the attendant was watching him. She was handing out garments as people skulked out into the hall. She handed him a garment. This one was yellow too. It was the same as the one he'd worn before, but it was not that one. He put it on and followed her. His knotted shoulders made bunches in the cloth. His sallow, ill-treated neck rose from the hemmed neck-hole to where his head rode in the air above his shoulders, its weight settling always implacably down. Like a puppet when one looks at it, he was for that moment more real than the things around him. Equally laughably obvious: he couldn't possibly be the center of anything and neither can you. ∎

Throughout my childhood I desperately wanted a horse, but my parents said we couldn't afford one. Awkwardly for them, when I was twelve my friend Emily, whose mother was on welfare, got a horse. It was a rescue horse, but a horse.

The day we first got drunk at thirteen, Emily and I took this horse, Rebel, for a walk. We'd both thrown up many times and were too fucked up to think about riding. The horse also had a heart condition. I can't remember if this factored into our decision. I know we three were all frail, walking slowly through the neighborhood, the horse saying nothing while we two humans talked about our shame.

In addition to the horse, Emily's family had two dogs, two cats, a raccoon, a descented skunk and innumerable guinea pigs who escaped and now lived and reproduced in the walls of her house like mice. The house was a real log cabin, built as a summer house on the bank of a pond. Her parents were divorced and her father lived in a trailer a few doors down. Once she brought me to his trailer while he was away to show me his stash of pornographic novels. I remember two sentences from the most shocking novel, *Pre-teen Sex Club*. The first sentence was, 'Jean's cunt itched.' A few pages later, when Jean is pretending to be asleep while her pre-teen son has sex with her, the son thinks to himself: 'Oh Mother, you are a no-good filthy slut.'

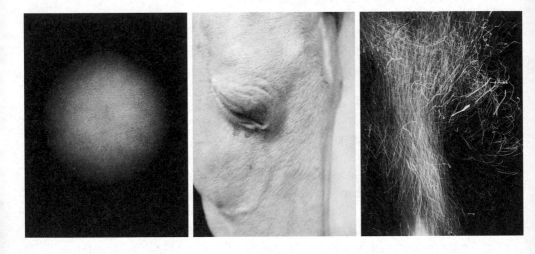

DAVID JIMÉNEZ

Emily's older brother, David, had severe developmental disabilities. He never learned to speak or dress himself. He was a big guy and it got hard to keep him at home as he developed a teenaged emotional life. On occasion, he violently defended himself against the people helping him. It was already clear he was headed for a home; he would die in one at twenty-eight. There is no good solution for some problems.

I was at the house once when this brother was riding the horse around the paddock while masturbating. From outside the fence his mother kept patiently, vainly asking him to stop. The horse walked round and round. The boy masturbated happily in his safe perch. ■

A LAST CHANCE
IN WHITEFISH

Adam O'Fallon Price

I was driving through Montana when I saw them standing on the shoulder: the young woman and the old man. Western Montana – where that famous big sky gives way to blue-green mountains in every direction, and the road begins to twist and rise and fall. But this was on a straight, downhill shot, and the smoke coming off their car was visible from a quarter-mile, so I had plenty of time to consider whether I was going to stop.

There weren't cell phones back then. This would have been the late eighties, I think, because I was driving that giant blue Mercedes 1974 SEL sedan, the only car I've ever really loved. If there had been cell phones, this story would be different. For one thing, it wouldn't have happened. I would have assumed they were waiting on a tow they'd already called, maybe at most I'd have called 911 and let the police know they should swing by. And, of course, today I wouldn't be driving around aimlessly with the entire world laid out before me like presents on Christmas morning, but that's a different thing. Back then, two people stuck on a stretch of lonely road was a real problem.

I stopped. It hadn't hurt, if I'm being completely honest, that as I got closer it became clear the woman was blond and pretty, wearing one of those impractical furry throw jackets, and that the flanneled man beside her was probably forty years her senior. I felt like the traveling salesman in one of those lame jokes about the farmer's daughter, only I wasn't a salesman – I taught high-school English on a Crow reservation outside Billings – and the man wasn't a farmer. He was a preacher, or so he said after they'd gotten in the car, and to make conversation I'd asked what they did.

This was also after I'd agreed to take them to Whitefish, nearly a hundred miles away, and I'd U-turned the car back up that long hill. She, riding shotgun, sighed and said, 'He's not a preacher, he's a sculptor.'

'Oh, yeah?'

'Yeah, a famous one,' she said, with a note of unmistakable pride.

He snorted. 'Hardly.'

'He has a piece in the Smithsonian.'

'Some garbage folk art exhibit.'

'Wait, what's your name?' I said.

He said nothing, so she answered for him. 'Zell Jeffers.'

The name rang a faint bell, or maybe it just sounded like someone famous. A grunt issued from the back seat, as though in protest at his name being spoken so casually. 'Hardly famous,' he said again, as I merged onto US-93 at Missoula. 'Famous people have cars that don't blow up in the middle of nowhere.'

'It could happen to anyone,' she said.

'But you ever notice,' he said, 'how this shit always happens to me.'

'People's cars break down.'

'You're my lucky charm,' he said, and she turned to the window. 'Anyway –' he caught my eyes in the rearview – 'thanks for the lift. I'll make it worth your while.'

'No need.'

'You said you were headed west, this is way out of your way.'

I'd said I was headed west, and it was true. I was planning to drop in on a girl I knew in Coeur d'Alene. But, also true: I wasn't sure if the girl still lived there, and I was about as much headed to Whitefish as anywhere. On my summer breaks, I drove all over the plains and upper Midwest, taking those little white cross ephedrine pills you could still buy at gas stations, humping around my big Minolta to shoot artless photos of crows standing in fields, drinking beer in dingy motels with a sense that something might happen, though it pretty much never did. I was a romantic, and like many romantics, I fancied myself some kind of artist, or rather, someone with an artistic soul – someone who one day might become an artist, if they lived their life in an artistic manner. In truth, I was pleased by the new possibilities my day suddenly contained with these two strange people in my car.

'What's your name,' said the woman. She was older than I'd first thought – older than I was, maybe thirty. Her hair was parted in the middle and she wore buckskin moccasin boots that came up over her jeans to mid-calf. She struck me as one of those late-hippie types you still ran into in the sticks, displaced in situation and time, better suited to 1968 than 1988, and so removed from modern culture that you couldn't tell if they knew the difference. 'I'm Molly. Like Malone.'

'Eugene.'

'Like O'Neill,' she said.

'Like Debs. Like Oregon,' sing-sang the voice from the back seat, punctuated by the light crack of a bottle being opened.

US-93 north was a flat, alternately four- and two-lane road that first passed Missoula, the bleak trailer-parked Missoula outskirts, then the Flathead Reservation, Flathead Lake, and past that, I knew from a previous ramble through these parts, Kalispell and Whitefish, and the jarring contrast of their tract housing and million-dollar lodges. Along the way, the Mission Mountains, white-capped in May, rose to the right of the car, and the increasingly beautiful landscape seemed to animate Molly in turn. She grew talkative about their lives, downright garrulous, and I could feel the figure behind us tensing at the sustained noise of her voice.

'We were headed over to Spokane to see Zell's daughter, but I never felt right about the trip. Too much bad juju from the start.'

Zell said, 'What's bad juju is always thinking everything is bad juju. It creates an atmosphere.'

'Something you're an expert in.'

'I don't deny it.'

'Well,' she said, 'let's just say there were signs, and I think the car breaking down was fortunate. I had a dream last night that we hit a patch of ice and skidded off the road, flipped down sideways into a ravine.'

Zell said, 'No ice in May.'

'It's a metaphor.'

'The reason,' Zell said, 'that she didn't want to go to Spokane, is that she and my daughter don't get along. My daughter thinks Molly here is using me for my fame and fortune. If she only knew.'

'I'm only in it for the sweetness and good conversation,' Molly said.

'Shut your mouth.'

'Hey,' I said. The car grew silent, but the harshness of the words hung in the air like a sour smell – like, in fact, the increasingly strong odor of whiskey emanating from the back seat. To dispel some of the atmosphere, as Zell had called it, I turned on the radio to a fuzzy AM station playing old sixties surf hits: Dick Dale and The Surfaris. The weirdness of the moment was amplified by the shimmying twang of reverb guitar in the background, and it seemed that this would be an important day in my life. Although maybe it didn't – maybe that's me assigning the feeling I would come to have about that day to my feelings at the time, if that makes sense, a significance freighted in after the fact.

Zell had gotten his way and Molly had hushed, turning her attention to the passing landscape out the window. She was a fascinating-looking person, in that rawboned Joni Mitchell mode. Hair so blond it was almost white, and skin so thin that on her temple you could see a pulsing blue vein, like a mountain road on a map, full of switchbacks. She said, with quiet stubbornness, 'Anyway, I think this whole thing was a blessing.'

Zell said, as though to the world, 'Oh, to be possessed of this woman's disposition! For every piece of bad luck to be good luck!'

'Oh, Jesus, you shut up,' said Molly. She turned to me, 'Enough with our bullshit, what do you do?'

I told them what I did, as briefly as I could.

She said, 'And you're from Philadelphia? How on earth did you wind up out here?'

How did people wind up anywhere? In my case, the answer was that after college I'd seen a life of safe boredom stretch out yawning before me – some version of graduate work (even – oof – law school), eventual marriage and mild-mannered suburbanization either in Delaware County where half my family lived, or in some other leafy Acela corridor locale. So when I came across a brochure in the student union for teaching in reservations out West, it seemed not like a calling or great moral enterprise, but an escape, the chance to reinvent myself somewhere completely different and exciting.

But where I'd wound up, a dumpy little duplex in Billings, did not feel that different or exciting, despite the ghostly blue mountains in the distance. My landlady and her yapping dachshund lived beneath me, and she beat her ceiling with a broom if I played music after eight. I still sometimes got a thrill from living what seemed like such an unusual life – but, in truth, the kids on the reservation weren't all that different from the same bored teenagers you found everywhere. They listened to metal and got high before class, and resented your authority like all high-school students, albeit with much greater historical cause. Driving home from the res every afternoon, I still had the sense of waiting for my life to happen.

After my quick precis, the old man said, 'Rumspringa, huh?'

'What?'

'That's what those, uh – the Amish call it. Go away for a year and get crazy.'

'I'm working on three years now. Thinking I might move out to LA.' As I talked, I realized that I'd taken on his clipped, macho manner of speech, and I understood that I wanted his approval, despite not knowing him, and despite disliking the little bit I'd seen so far. It's always been a failing of mine, looking for respect from people who are themselves not worthy of it. 'It's not a rum-whatever.'

I was close to angry, I realized, but Molly's hand patting my leg pulled me out of it. Intended, it seemed, as reassurance not to worry about whatever Zell was saying, it was still her hand on my leg, and a thrill ran up through my groin into the lower part of my gut.

'You'll go back.' His giant head appeared again in the rearview, but this time he wasn't looking at me. Despite the enormity of the Missions out the passenger side, he was seated behind me, staring out at a dense wall of trees beside the lake as though tracking something out there in them. He said, 'It's like churches. You go back to the one you were raised in. I hated the Catholic Church for forty years, but now I say my rosary.'

Molly said, 'He does, every day.'

'You can't get away from anything. You spend your whole life running and you realize you ran around the world and you're back where you were born.'

Molly said, 'So depressing.'

'But true.'

I said, 'You were born in Whitefish?'

'No, Maryland. But I am my father, it's a goddamned nightmare.'

We drove on in silence, with her hand either on or not on my leg. I'm old enough not to trust my memory anymore. Things get added and blurred and combined, often in ways that make everything more logical. At some point during the drive, there was a leg and a hand, but that's about all I can vouchsafe. The dialogue, of course, is almost entirely invented, though true to the spirit and tone.

B y the time we got to Whitefish, the old man was drunk. He'd probably already been about halfway there when I picked them up and just finished the job in my back seat. He said it was imperative that he get to a place called the Stone Rooster, but he couldn't seem to direct me there. Eventually, I rolled down the window and asked a bearded fellow, who pointed and said a few blocks that way up the hill, near the lodges.

He said, 'Is that Zell Jeffers?'

'Yeah,' I said.

'No shit.' His expression was unreadable, and that good feeling I'd had when I picked them up returned. Here I was, ferrying a famous – if drunk and irascible – artist around, enjoying the possibly erotic attention of his wife; who knew what might happen later? If every day could be like this, filled with chance meetings and secret knowledge ... this feeling, I realized, was what I wanted all the time, was why I'd moved out West in the first place. I'd wanted to experience something new, but more than that, I'd wanted a kind of wild uncertainty and to live daily with the prospect that, good or bad, anything might happen. Of course, to have that feeling, anything sometimes had to happen, and it hadn't for a while.

The Stone Rooster was the restaurant bar of an old resort hotel. Around two in the afternoon, during the off-season, there was hardly anyone there, just an older couple silently eating eggs and bacon in the corner while they read the newspaper. The bartender looked up from a book as the entry bell tinkled. Zell hobbled over and said, 'Johnny here?'

The bartender shook his head and looked back down at the paper. Zell said, 'He coming in tonight?'

'No, tonight's Lee.'

'When's he coming in?'

'How should I know?'

Zell brought something out of his pocket and laid it on the bar. We were standing behind Zell, a little to the side, so I couldn't see what it was, but it was nevertheless clear from the bartender's reaction, the way all humor and expression drained from his face, that it was a gun.

The bartender said, 'I honestly don't know when he's coming in. You want me to call him?'

'Just when I thought common courtesy was dead.'

The bartender shuffled down the bar to where a plastic cordless sat on a shelf. I moved a little to the left and saw that I'd been right. On the bar top, the old man had plunked down an equally old gun. With its ivory handle and long silver barrel, it looked like something from a western, although I know as little now about guns as I did then.

I heard Molly mutter *Shit*, not with fear or even surprise, but with the tired inflection of a woman who'd dealt with the same routine ten times already this year alone. The couple in the corner somehow seemed not to have noticed, or maybe this kind of thing went on all the time in Whitefish, was a normal way of settling a dispute.

The bartender spoke into the phone, glancing up at Zell now and then. He said, 'Johnny's down in Colorado right now.'

'Who're you talking to, then?'

'His wife.'

'I bet. Listen, you tell him the next time I see him he'd better have that money he owes me, or I'm gonna shoot him in the knee. Tell him I brought the gun, so he knows I'm serious.'

The bartender repeated the words, though they'd been spoken loudly enough that surely the person on the other end had heard. The bartender hung up, and Zell said, 'Okay, give me a Jack rocks and whatever those two want.'

Molly said, 'Just a water.'

Everyone was waiting on me, I realized. 'A beer, I guess?'

'A beer, he guesses.'

The bartender got us our drinks and we moved to a table by the long window that looked out onto the streets of Whitefish. I expected to see police lights tearing down the road any second and became nervous about the little white pills in my pocket, even though they were legal. Molly didn't look worried, though. She sipped her water through a straw while staring at Zell, who slouched into his chair at such an angle that he almost had to reach up for his drink.

'Shouldn't we leave?' I asked.

'Why, 'cause of old Chekhov, here?' He patted the gun which he'd returned to somewhere in the recesses of his flannel jacket.

He looked at me appraisingly, and I said, 'Yeah, I get it. The gun on the mantel that has to go off at some point.'

'Not only that, but it makes things happen, drives the plot along. Gets surly bartenders to pick up the phone.'

I said, 'You should call it Chandler, then,' which felt pretty clever to me but drew no acknowledgment. 'Isn't he going to call the cops?'

'Hell, no. He knows I'm old friends with Brickley.'

'Sheriff Brickley,' clarified Molly.

'Brickley's not gonna bring me up on pulling out a gun. That's barely a crime, anyway.'

'Threatening someone with a gun isn't a crime?'

'Depending on who you are, no. Quit worrying and drink your beer.' We sat silent for a minute or two. I noticed that there was music playing, the Eagles, 'One of These Nights'. Either it had been playing when we'd walked in, or the bartender had put it on after their little showdown. Zell said, 'You're a worrier, huh? My son's that way. Bad worrier, they got him on all kinds of meds.'

Molly said, 'Because a childhood spent watching scenes like that –' she pointed at the bar – 'fucked him up.'

'Shut your mouth,' he said again.

She shrugged. 'Not like you don't know it.'

'It's getting so,' he said, squinting into his drink, then theatrically raising his gaze to meet hers, 'I'm just not having fun anymore.'

'Feel free to leave any time you want.' She looked at me. 'Zell likes to act like everything's his, but we've been together eight years, common law. And I've worked that whole time.'

He laughed. 'Some work, ferrying Mexican skunkweed around the Badlands.'

'How much did your artwork bring in last year?'

'Not shit,' he laughed.

I was wondering, at that point, how I could reasonably extricate myself from the situation. It seemed I was no longer a temporary chauffeur, I'd become some kind of powerless referee, an unwitting witness to their union's demise. There was a certain lurid interest in it, but the stunt with the gun had charged everything with the ugly undertone of potential violence.

I pushed up from the table. 'You know where the bathroom is here?'

Zell said, 'You're not thinking about leaving us are you?'

'No.'

'I wouldn't blame you if you were. We're a bit of a load right now.'

'*We*,' said Molly.

He ignored her. 'But the house is only about ten minutes up the hill behind here. I've got money there to pay you, can't give you shit unless you get us there.'

'Sure, of course,' I said.

'Thank you, Eugene,' Molly said, again squeezing my leg.

In the bathroom, I bent over the basin splashing water on my face and looking at myself in the mirror, since that seemed like what a person was supposed to do at times like these. What were times like these? When a crazy old gun nut's common-law drug-runner wife was coming on to you: times like those? I had a full head of hair back then, unruly and thick, and I smoothed the water from my face up into it, slicking it back a little. The thing was, I knew if I walked out, I'd always wonder how the story ended, what might have happened. Looking back to that time from where I am now, I wish I'd had even more of that resolve. But I had enough at that moment, at least, to return to the table and say, 'All right, let's go.'

The way to Zell and Molly's house was up a steep grade, a barely paved joke road that turned to gravel halfway. Molly was saying how bad it was when it snowed here, and Zell, riding shotgun now, was saying how much he liked it because no one could get in or out. I said, 'How long have you lived here?'

Zell said, 'Going on twenty years. I built the place when I still had a career. Used to draw a steady income down at the university. It's a monument to how nothing goes the way you expect it will.'

Molly said, 'Isn't everything, though?'

'It illustrates the issue with particular force.'

Their long, rutted driveway ended at a house that was, surprisingly and a bit disappointingly, not the rustic log cabin I'd anticipated, but rather a semi-modernist structure. A wrap-around balcony bisected the floors, and the walls were mostly made of windows. Before I'd even turned off the engine, Zell had already gotten out and slammed his door. I let Molly out of the back.

'What a gentleman,' said Zell without turning around. Molly's eyes were fixed on me, less with desire than a kind of desperate pleading, though I didn't know what she would have had me do. 'You want a drink?' he said. 'I'm having one.'

'Shocking,' she said.

'Come on,' said Zell. 'I gotta get you that gas money anyway.'

I'd been impressed by the architectural skill on display, but as I got up to the door, I saw how run-down the place really was: a tall side window broken and covered with cardboard, paint blistered away, a loose board hanging over the porch by a single rusty nail. The inside of the house was surprisingly dark given the number of windows. It was the trees – they pressed up against the glass with a dense avidity that seemed indecent. On the walls were all sorts of animal heads, Gothic in the noon-time twilight. I tried to imagine living in this place and couldn't, but I've never had much of an imagination.

Zell came back from wherever he'd gone with a bottle and three glasses. He filled them, drank his in a swallow and refilled it. Past his shoulder, at the far end of a dining room lined with stacked boxes, was a window looking out on the rear of the house. I noticed what appeared to, but couldn't, be a horde advancing from the forest.

Zell turned, 'Oh, that. Well, you might as well see my shit, you came all the way here.'

He led me through the dining room, past an unspeakably filthy kitchen, and out onto a deck overlooking an enormous backyard. Although it was really more of a huge clearing in the forest, and in this clearing stood dozens of sculptures, upward of a hundred. They were metal, a dark pewter gray, terrifying half-human and half-monster shapes. You tried to find the equilibrium between the two forms, but as soon as you did, the shape seemed to assume either man or beast, and the meaning slipped back and forth like mercury.

'Wow,' I said.

'Twenty years of work, and I think about melting them all down at least once a day.'

'Why?'

He looked out over them, chin jutted. 'The danger in making things –' he began and paused, and when he spoke again, he spoke slowly, almost in a different register than he had all day; I couldn't tell if he was thinking harder about what he was saying, or if the whiskey had finally hit him full force – 'the danger in trying to do anything meaningful with your life, is that it isn't enough, maybe isn't anything, and you know it. You're better off not doing anything. At least that way preserves the illusion that if you wanted to, you could do something that mattered.'

He turned away from the tableau and his normal demeanor returned. 'Anyway, they aren't worth shit, Smithsonian or not. Not worth shit if no one's buying.' I tried to imagine the person who would want one of these things in or near their house. To see them in a museum would be one thing, to live with one, quite another. I was searching for what to say, but he drained his glass and said, 'I'll get your money.'

He hobbled inside, barking something. I looked back over the dead army below me and shuddered. I suddenly very much wished I was currently on my way to Coeur d'Alene. I was learning things I didn't want to know. A hand touched my shoulder from behind, and I turned. Molly clinked my glass.

We drank, and she said quietly, 'I have to get out of here.'

'Yeah?'

'You don't understand, I love him, but it's going to kill me. Either he is, or living with him is, one of the two.'

I said, 'You want to go with me?' and it was unclear, I think to both of us, whether I was inviting her to go with me, or clarifying if that's what she was asking. For a moment, she considered me, standing there in my jeans and unscuffed work boots, with my stupid wallet chain. Instead of answering, she bent forward and kissed me. It was a long, slow kiss, not hard, gentle and pure in its way. What I mean is it wasn't raunchy, it almost felt chaste.

'What would we do?' she said.

'I don't know. I was going to go to LA soon. We could go there.'

'I've been there. It was nice.' Was that a demurral or the expression of a desire to go back? Again, it was unclear – or rather, in my memory it's unclear. Maybe it was clear in the moment and then blurred by what happened next.

The loud bang of a gun knocked us apart, and I distinctly recall dropping my glass. It rolled slowly off the deck and landed with a thunk in the brown grass of the yard. Molly ran inside and I followed close behind. We went down the dark hall, to a closed door at the end. She knocked, and Zell called a singsong, 'It's lo-ocked.'

'Put down the gun and come out.'

'I saw you out there!'

'Open the door!'

'I'm done with this shit. Today's the day.'

'You've told me today's the day a hundred times.'

'Well, I must have been lying, but today really is.'

I asked her if she wanted me to call the cops, and Zell, who must have been closer than I'd imagined to the door, yelled, 'Get him out of here.'

'No, he's nice!'

'I saw how nice you think he is, I saw it the whole drive up here!'

She looked at me. Her face was like a mask only slightly larger than the real face it concealed. Her eyes were that watery blue that almost isn't blue, just the suggestion of it. She said, softer, almost lullingly, 'Zell.'

The door unlocked. After a moment, she opened it to reveal a room darker than the hall. Zell was seated on a straight-backed chair, holding the gun in his lap. We waded into the room – that's what it felt like, the damp air almost unbreathable from the choking ammonia of cat piss. An orange longhair darted past us into the hall, and a tabby yowled from under the bed, where it had hidden when the gun went off. Speaking of the gun, Zell had presumably shot at the ceiling, but it was impossible to tell where he'd shot, since, at a glance, there were at least five other bullet holes. It occurred to me that I was standing before a drunk, armed man who'd seen me kissing his wife. I credit sheer, idiot youth with the astounding presumption that no ill would befall me in that room.

Molly said, 'Give me the gun.'

He said, 'Eugene, what do you think I should do?'

'What?'

'I mean, we don't get much outside perspective here. What's my play? I'm washed up, this woman here hates me. We're running out of money. I'm sixty-seven and my kidneys don't work right anymore. What's my play?'

'I don't know. Quit drinking and move somewhere else?'

'Ha!'

Molly said, 'Let's just go to your sister's. She can help out.'

'I'll tell you what.' He handed me the gun, butt first, and I took it automatically, to disarm him. 'Why don't you shoot me?'

Molly said, 'Zell, come on.'

'No, listen. I hate these scenes too. It's embarrassing. You know I'm a coward. And I wouldn't ask you to do it. But Eugene could.'

I said, 'I'm not shooting you.'

'Wait, hear me out.' He pulled open his flannel a little, revealing a thatch of gray hair. His head was monstrous, overgrown, like the head of a huge dog you might see tied up in a backyard some hot summer day, grinning in its misery. 'The way it would go, Brickley would be the one to investigate, and Molly would tell him I'd done it. You just wipe the gun and put it in my hand. Brickley'd have it wrapped up in about five minutes, and there's no one who wouldn't breathe a little easier, don't think I don't know that.

'Eugene, I like you. I think you're a decent type. There's three grand here, Molly knows where it is. I was going to give you a hundred for the ride. Three grand to do everyone a favor. Maybe you and Molly could go somewhere and start over with the rest of the money. I wouldn't begrudge it, honestly.'

The gun was less heavy than I would have imagined. I had it in my hand, pointed at the floor. Chekhov, what an asshole. 'I'm not going to shoot you.'

'Why not?'

'I guess I just don't want to be someone who's killed someone.'

'You're going to wind up being someone you don't want to be, one way or the other.'

'No.'

'Come on, do it.'

This is the moment I've replayed in the decades since, hundreds of times. Him sitting there, shirt half open, Molly beside me, the smell of cat piss and cordite in the air. I don't know how long it was, but for at least a few long seconds, I truly considered raising the gun and firing. Shooting him in the chest and waiting to see what happened. I believed his offer to be sincere. But the thing I remember really giving me pause – beyond the simple fact of having to kill another human being – was when I glanced again at the bullet holes in the ceiling and realized this was something that had happened before, some version of it. Not just Zell throwing these suicidal fits, but I wondered if I was the first fool who'd found them broken down on the side of the road. Was this some *Who's Afraid of Virginia Woolf?* melodrama they played out for fun every now and then? Had there been other young men with cars, other legs, other whispered conversations about going somewhere far away, other gentle kisses overlooking Zell's nightmare statuary? Molly's white face, hanging in the dimness like the moon on a summer night, offered no clue.

I turned away from him and away from Molly. I walked out of the room, down the hall, and set the gun on top of a bookshelf, where it might take him a few minutes to find it. I drove down their driveway and the house disappeared behind me. I turned onto a fire road and sat there for a while, waiting for my breath to return, and while I did – this is so unbelievable that once again I doubt my memory – the biggest blacksnake I've ever seen leisurely coiled its way across the trail into a shadowy patch of bramble.

I drove back down that mountain road. Outside, it was the same bright May day it had been, but the color felt grainy and washed out. I didn't have the taste for my trip anymore. The girl in Coeur d'Alene, or rather the possibility of anything happening with the girl in Coeur d'Alene, seemed utterly fictive, fanciful. I'd been somehow disabused by the day's events.

Living in Montana, teaching on a reservation, fantasizing about women who may or may not have remembered me, taking road trips to nowhere and photos of nothing: what was all of this about, besides indulging some fantasy of freedom and the romantic image of myself as a free spirit? And simultaneously true: though it was all smoke, it was also my life. I'd been there almost three years already – how long before that fantasy, that smoke, took shape into an existence, hardening over time into the real thing? The real version of all this light romance, the version five or ten or fifteen years down the line, would not be romantic at all, and I felt myself faced with a kind of last chance. I was, of course, only twenty-five, but I was the kind of twenty-five-year-old who felt old at twenty-five, who saw last chances everywhere.

I remember the sun setting behind me as I drove down a highway that, in either direction, had always seemed to lead away from home, and now only seemed to lead back from where I'd come.

Shortly thereafter, I put in my notice with the school and my landlady. The possessions in my apartment, boxed and loaded into a U-Haul trailer, were shockingly and heartbreakingly few. I made the drive back to Philly in three days, camping out in KOA areas in Nebraska and Indiana. I stayed at my parents' house for the rest of that long summer, and got a job at a private girls' school. My wife taught history at that school, and we began dating that first year. My ex-wife, I should say. My ex-wife, with whom I have two children; my ex-wife who left me after nearly twenty years; my ex-wife, whose father, stricken with dementia, I still visit every week in the nursing home. There's a lot more to that story, of course, to those decades, but the basic contours are clear and simple, and not very different from what I'd expected and feared would happen when I graduated college. Maybe I knew myself then better than I thought I did.

Sometimes I still think about that highway, the old man and the girl standing there like messengers with terrible news, or like the terrible news itself. And in my memories of that strange day, I often wonder what would have happened if I'd done Zell the favor he'd asked for. Impossible to know, but I think things would have gone more or less just as he'd said.

It isn't as though I think that that one moment in that dark bedroom was the moment where everything might have been different. Maybe it was and maybe it wasn't. Maybe the old man was right, and no matter what you do you wind up in the same place.

It isn't as though I hate my life. But still, I wish I'd shot him. ∎

STILLS

Robbie Lawrence

Introduction by Colin Herd

At the start of this pandemic, I had three living grandparents, and now I have one. The poet Kwame Dawes writes of 'the idea of the poem as caught in that "still point" between time present, time past, and time future'. These stills by Robbie Lawrence, rephotographed from moving pictures made by his grandmother, perform just such a *still point.*

Ah, the Forth bridges. When I was a first-year undergraduate in Edinburgh, I used to visit my great-aunt in Queensferry every couple of weeks for lunch or tea. We had a soft spot for each other. I once as a child read a poem at her birthday party. It was in a little restaurant where my gran sometimes worked, called the Bakehouse, so I'm assuming it had been a bakery. It had a big crevice under the stairs.

The amber light in these photographs feels like still-point light. Amber, neither stop nor go. Starting in 1962, the poet Jackson Mac Low made a long series of poems using a chart of descriptions of light over twenty-six years. The first light poem, for Iris, includes these lines: 'Citrine light / kineographic light / the light of a Kitson lamp / kindly light'.

My great-aunt would cook lentil soup, and she made amazing pancakes, but this period also coincided with increasing disorientation and confusion which ended up being diagnosed as Alzheimer's. She would talk about a blue light, which gave her a lot of anxiety, and us, too, because we assumed it was the gas on her hob, but the blue light sometimes came from the sink. She always asked if I had a girlfriend, and I always said 'no' and smiled. I stood on the stairs to read the birthday poem, which everyone greeted, of course, with kindness. It wasn't watching my cousin play a schools final at Hampden.

I've never curled, not in that way anyway. The choreography of bodies on the ice feels familiar, this elegant sense of slight dexterous flail to keep balance, to stay upright. I'm reminded a little of the work of Édouard Levé, the writer and photographer who got people dressed in business attire to position themselves into tableaux of stills from rugby matches and pornographic films. The tableaux in these images are more subtle, just a protruding of the wings, an anticipatory bend in the knee.

Speaking of knees, a part of the body that's largely lost to fashion is that small space between short and knee-length sock, that little cashew-nut curl of goose-pimpled elastic-tattooed skin. I'm trying to recall being involved in legendary snowball fights but I can't. I mean I remember plenty of snowy days. I remember my brother shatteringly putting his arm through the window in our school canteen in a rushed effort to wipe off something someone had written about him in the condensation. I remember an ice-skating disco where I just went round and round and round. They always played the song 'Deeply Dippy' by Right Said Fred.

Dawes continues his characterisation of the *still point*:

> Poetry is, indeed, a form that carries us to unknown places even when those places are known through memory. The relooking that poetry represents is thus an encounter with the unknown, and one that eventually proves to be necessary and exciting.

There's so much glass between us and Mercedes. I think this must be Mercedes, anyway, the polar bear that lived in Edinburgh Zoo for twenty-five years, having survived being shot in Canada. Reinforced Edinburgh Zoo glass, a camcorder lens, a still camera lens and also a laptop screen. I, too, want to nuzzle my face in my paw with embarrassment, a kind of shy memory. My gran and grandad celebrated a joint eightieth birthday at Edinburgh Zoo. We walked around the zoo and then had a meal in their function suite, with a disco afterwards. Why do I always remember the discos? It was weird having a disco so close to the pandas, penguins, bantengs, lions, chimpanzees, etc. I think Mercedes had died by then, so she was spared that at least.

Dawes writes of the *still point* of poetry in terms of comfort, especially at times when 'so many lives I know have been strained by what have become ordinary tragedies'. I have to be honest and say that comfort doesn't always sit that comfortably with me. Don't we want to shake things up with the uncomfortable, the discomforting, the curling stone under the sofa cushion, the blue light in the sink? Looking at Robbie Lawrence's intensely intimate photographs, though, caught in an overlap of memory, imagination and invention, caught between the present, the past and the future, I feel that the momentary comfort of these images doesn't close off the possibility of flux and change, but instead opens up pockets in the midst of them; pockets we can put our hands in and shift our weight to the balls of our feet. It's my gran's birthday on Saturday; I'll spare her the poetry reading. ■

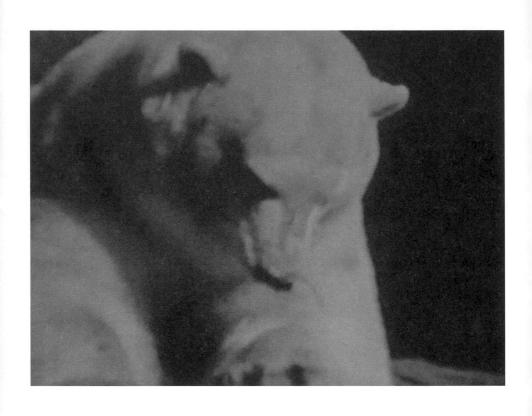

Read more for less
Try 3 issues of *Literary Review*
for only £5

Subscribe: +44 (0) 1778 395 165 • www.literaryreview.co.uk

USE CODE 'GRANTA'

ARCMANORO NILES
I Want To Believe Even If Life Doesn't Play Fair (Love Was Never Blind But I Was), 2020
Courtesy of the artist and Lehmann Maupin, New York, Hong Kong, Seoul and London

MBIU DASH

Okwiri Oduor

We were all there the day Mr Man came to town, driving that blister-coloured tin car. It looked like he had scrounged the dumpsters for scraps, like he had welded them together under a flaying sun, building an automobile out of tractor parts and posho mill parts and old radiator and washing machine parts. We thought to ourselves, 'A man like this must have a good story lodged beneath his tongue.' We knew that we wanted him to stay for as long as it took to get that story out.

It was the first of December, Epitaph Day in our town. That's the day of the year that we set aside for remembering our dearly departed. In the morning, we went to Our Lady of Lourdes, and Father Jude Thaddeus called each of our dead by name, and we blinked tears into our canvas shoes and swallowed the Communion host and said to each other, 'Take heart, my dear, take heart.'

And afterwards, we went to the brewhouse, and Mama Chibwire dipped into her barrels and handed out mugs of mead. That's what we were doing when Mr Man came to town. We were sipping on mead and sniffling into our sleeves. Thinking of the way Salama used to cut chunks off the cow's rump right while it grazed on the field, thinking of Aminata's funny skulking walk, thinking of GodblessAmen's way with cane rats, how they followed him every which way he went, like he was the Pied Piper, how the neighbourhood children took to saying that

GodblessAmen himself looked like a cane rat, and when they said this, the grown folk started to see it too, and we all believed that no doubt GodblessAmen had once been a cane rat himself and no doubt he would turn into one again when he was done with this wearisome life.

That's exactly how it happened in the end. GodblessAmen was riding his motorcycle when he got waylaid by a boda boda thief and received a machete blow to the neck. Someone telephoned the police. They arrived to find him no longer a man, just a mangled rat trying to dig itself into the murky ground. The police were frothing at the mouth. They would not believe that a dying man had just up and turned himself into a cane rat. They smacked the bystanders with clubs, saying, 'You dare waste the government's time?'

We were at the brewhouse that Epitaph Day, and we were sipping on mead, and thinking of all the ones we had lost. Then Mr Man drove by in his tin car, squinting, forehead scrunched, looking like he owed us a story. Mama Chibwire poured him a mug, and we all scooted over to make room for him and for that wretched soul that followed him around. And Philomena sat in his lap because she was already drunk and when Philomena is drunk she's truly mannerless – she will climb atop of tables and piss in soda bottles, or she will grab a hog by its corkscrew tail and drag it, grunting and tottering, across the town, until the apothecary runs out of her wood cottage, waving a cast-iron pan, saying, 'Philomena Nanjala, let that poor devil go or I will wreck your medulla oblongata!'

Mr Man gulped down his drink, mouth twisted on account of the floral notes of the mead – the lilacs and the lantanas that the honeybees had suckled. Or perhaps just on account of the mead's cloying sweetness. He did not seem to like what Philomena was doing on him, either. She was writhing, her eyes closed, looking like a woman deep in the throes of childbirth. She acted like she was doing something sensual, like she was trying to seduce the poor fellow, trying to make him say, 'Haki ya nani, you're finishing me!' But us, we knew the truth. She was only trying to feel for his wallet, to learn how fat its contents were, so she could make up her mind whether he was worth her time or not. We were horrified at her guts. We said, 'Philomena Nanjala, behave yourself!'

Philomena's sister, Petronilla, was there with us too. She grew vexed. She jumped up from her stool, grabbed Philomena and tossed her out the window. Philomena fell into the puddle below, where she promptly blacked out.

We felt ashamed, like we had let Mr Man see us with snot smeared across our cheeks, or with holes in our bloomers. We felt we ought to apologize for Philomena's gaudy behavior. So we gave Mr Man ingratiating smiles, and complimented him on his shirt, which read *United Colors of Benetton*.

'Where are you from?' Mama Chibwire asked, filling Mr Man's mug.

He pointed over his shoulder with his gnarled-up thumb, towards the wispy, mint-coloured horizon. We wondered to ourselves if he meant just over the valley, or if he meant a place like Sudan or Manitoba or Kyoto. A man like that really could have come from anywhere. And with that wretched soul, too, following him everywhere like a haggard shadow. We looked at it, all curled up at Mr Man's feet. Where had Mr Man picked it up? Had an old hag given him the evil eye? Had a beggar asked for a coin, and then cursed him when he'd refused?

We looked pitifully at Mr Man.

'Stay,' we said to him. 'Stay for as long as you want.'

Me, I always thought of my mama on Epitaph Day. Now I wanted to gulp down a mug of mead in her honour. I wanted to pour some on the ground and say, 'Dottie Nyairo, you old scoundrel.' But Mama Chibwire wouldn't let me drink any mead. She said, 'Mbiu Dash, you're only *thirteen*.'

They made a mule out of me every chance they got. Everyone in the town did. They said, 'I see you're headed towards the marketplace, Mbiu Dash, be a good girl and take this bag of charcoal with you to the maize-roaster.' They said, 'What's an orphan like you running around for? You've got no place to go, and no people to see either. Here, scrub this bucketful of bed sheets. And mind, I'll be checking your pockets later, so don't think you can pinch any of the Omo.' They said, 'Mbiu Dash, hop on over and fetch the apothecary. Tell her that the rabbit keeper got that dirty thing of his stuck inside maid's hole again.'

When they had things for me to do, no one gave a squirrel's tail that I was thirteen. And when I was darting through the streets, knocking on their doors, saying, 'Please-please-please you've got to let me in before they catch me,' no one minded that I was thirteen either. They only tugged at their curtains, and said, 'Not my problem.'

Well, let me ask you, whose problem was it, then, that the police and the preacher men and the busboys wouldn't leave me alone? That they were always trying to sneak up on me, trying to stuff their fists in my mouth and do me the dirty? Whose problem was it that there were throwaway kids like me all over town, hiding in the gutters because no one wanted to see their grimy faces, stealing dried sardines from the fishmonger's stall, and running, constantly running, so as not to get dragged into the alleyways?

You're only thirteen. Fair enough. But I had seen much since that day my mama robbed the bank. This made me *big* thirteen, the type to be able to drink mead on Epitaph Day if I wanted. Still, Mama Chibwire slapped my hand if I reached for any of it. She gave me bone soup instead, and not even salted bone soup. I sipped glumly and I thought of my mama robbing the bank, how she laughed and laughed until no more sound came out of her throat.

Every Epitaph Day, Sospeter Were took out his PA system and played 'Vunja Mifupa', and we all spilled out of the brewhouse and did the chini-kwa-chini dance for our dead ones. We thought of how someday it would be us gone, and how some other people would be the ones twisting themselves and turning themselves upside down and inside out for us. It was a sweet thought, one that made our toes curl with glee. To be dead someday, and missed, and held tenderly by those we'd left behind – that was our greatest aspiration in Mapeli Town.

I got up too, to go dance for my mama. But the townspeople shook their heads at me and said, 'Mbiu Dash, you had best sit here and keep our guest company.'

I clicked my tongue to the roof of my mouth. 'Look what you did,' I said to Mr Man, when everyone else was gone.

'You like to dance?' he asked.

'What type of question is that? Everyone likes to dance.'

'Well, dance for me then I see.'

And I curled my lips. I was *big* thirteen. I knew what men were like. I said, 'Don't speak such mud to me. You think I'm a puppy dog, to do things for you just because you asked?'

Mr Man frowned, chastised.

I said, 'Why don't you ask *him* to dance for you?'

I was pointing at the wretched soul at his feet. It was a boy. Well, what was left over after the boy's boyhood was plucked away. He was all shrunken and empty and limp, like a squishy rubber toy. He wore an ivy cap, plaid shirt and corduroy trousers. He had glass shards for eyes, cobalt-coloured, sparkling even in the muted light of the brewhouse.

'Who is he?' I asked Mr Man.

'That's my son Magnanimous.'

Mr Man pushed his brew mug over to me, and said that I could have as much of his mead as I liked. I knew that a gesture like that was awfully suspicious. A grown chap like him, trying to intoxicate a young girl? I said, 'Shame on you, Mr Man.'

Then I got up and left, jumping out the side window so that none of the dancing townspeople would see and make me stay. I stumbled over Philomena, who was still lying in a muddy pool. I squatted down beside her. I studied her face, memorizing the arch of her eyebrows, the curve of her cheekbones, the bridge of her nose. I pushed her lips back and studied the inside of her mouth. Her gums were orange like a drying river, like henna on the fingernails of the women who sold baobab seeds outside the town mosque. A praying mantis hopped onto the sharp edge of her chin. I flicked it away before it could crawl higher, into her nostril. Then I lay down in the crook of Philomena's arm, with my ear pressed to her chest. I listened. It sounded like a seashell in there. White noise.

I pinched my eyes shut and pretended that Philomena was my mama. I pretended that it was the old days, before my mama ever robbed the bank. I pretended that my mama came home from work, and that we ate coconut rice with curried chicken, and that I had rubbed her sore back with oil of calendula and peppermint prescribed by the apothecary. And now we were lying together in the bed that we shared, my mama's soft snores making the chiffon canopy above us tremble.

My mama worked as a tooth doctor. Each evening, I ironed her white scrubs and set them ready for her. Now they dangled on a hanger behind the bedroom door. Sometimes, in the afternoons, she came to fetch me from school. I would find her standing by the barbed-wire fence, wearing her scrubs and a bear-fur trapper hat that she once found in a Moscow flea market. She would be smiling coyly, her eyes glowing in the sun, her pockets bulging with sweets.

My mama was not finicky like other tooth doctors. She always let me eat as much Goody Goody and Chupa Chups as I wanted. And she never once made me brush my teeth before bed. We had an understanding: I could ruin my teeth, perforate them with holes big enough to lose five-shilling coins inside, and she would patch them up for me with silver amalgam someday.

Every evening, as we lay in bed together, I chewed on bonbons and ball gums and gobstoppers. I chewed them until my jaws ached. I chewed them until the flax of the pillowcase stuck to my face. I chewed them and stared out our bedroom window, watching as men hobbled by, hawking a type of rhubarb which gave a person's virility back to them, and as women wheeled handcarts filled with sour flatbread and canisters of camel's milk. Busboys clambered onto the roofs of their fifty-seaters and lay there, smoking Lucky Strikes and singing 'I Shot the Sheriff'.

And my mama, she was lost inside herself, surrounded by a clammy, half-fragrant, half-pungent devil-wind that spun fast and flung rotted tonsils and misaligned jaws and Kalashnikov rifles at her.

'What are you doing?' someone asked.

I opened my eyes and was dismayed to find that I was not in the flat that my mama and I had once shared, but rather, in a puddle, cradling a drunken woman's head, pretending like she was my mama. Mr Man was watching me. He leaned out the window, with his mug of mead pressed to his hairy bottom lip, and with that wretched soul – that leftover boy Magnanimous – clinging diagonally across his body like a satchel.

'Nothing,' I said, and got up, and began to walk away.

'Wait,' Mr Man called. 'Wait, please.' And he scrambled to jump out of that brewhouse side window, same as I had just done.

I looked over my shoulder and saw that the townspeople were dancing a little ways off, their limbs melting in the heat like sticks of butter. They were drunk, every last one of them, and now they tottered, and they contorted themselves, and they hooked onto each other like parts of a chain-link fence.

I knew peril when I saw it. And here it was – a godforsaken man, prowling about, trying to ensnare a throwaway girl. He knew full well that the entire town had lost its mind to Mama Chibwire's mead. He knew that he could do anything to me no problem, there weren't any witnesses.

I said to myself, 'Mbiu Dash, you witless dunce, don't just stand there!'

I took off running towards the yellowwood trees. I quickly lost Mr Man – he did not know the way through the clock tower, or the boatyard, or the old cemetery, or the schoolhouse. Now I was in the town, and I went from window to window, peeking in. That's what I did on most days – pressed my face to dusty panes and squinted, watching as the townspeople drank masala tea and listened to *Je, Huu Ni Ungwana?* on the radio.

I started peeking through windows after I lost my mama. I was full of fear that I would wake up someday and find that everyone else was gone too. That I was *truly* alone. So, I watched the townspeople through their windows, to make sure that they were all still there, and that their hearts were all still pounding in their chests.

Currently, no one was home. The entire town was at the Epitaph Day dance by the brewhouse. I looked inside the empty houses, and it occurred to me that absence was just as meaningful to observe as presence. Each of the houses had its own muffled vivacity: shadows climbing up the walls, sitting in the rafters, chewing khat. Mice hobbling out of cracks and rolling like bowling balls across cement floors. And the ghosts of the dearly departed, returning briefly. Sitting in rocking chairs to darn threadbare coats. Swirling soups of pig's feet that were simmering on unattended stoves. Writing letters to loved ones they had left behind. Saying, *In the long of night, I walk the navy sky and count the stars with my own hand, naming each after you.*

Mr Man came driving in his jalopy, sticking his head out the window, saying, 'Wait, please!'

I took off running again. Past the tin houses that crinkled in the heat. Past the fields of bristle-grass and juniper bushes and sunflowers. Past the papyrus reeds and sycamores and wattle trees. Up the hill that sometimes wobbled on fatigued feet. To the vulgar house where my darling lived.

There was a rickety gate flanked by stone angels with severed heads. A yard full of tangled balls of thorn trees and wild flowers and barbed wire and stiff yellow grass. An awning, double doors, a chimney. I pressed my face to the windowpane and stared into her kitchen. Fruit flies darted over the wicker basket on the table, inside which a speckled mango decayed. A bird smacked against the pendant lamp hanging near my head. It was a rufous-naped lark. Its dull eyes glazed over in a momentary daze. Then it got its wits back and lurched away, leaving a tuft of tawny feathers on the stained glass.

Where was she, my darling? I started to panic. What if she had gone outside, and got caught by Mr Man? What if he had stuffed his fist in her mouth and dragged her into an alley and done her the dirty?

'Ayosa Ataraxis Brown!' I yelled, turning away from her kitchen. I looked through another window. She was not there, at the groaning staircase where she sometimes sat. I ran around to the butterfly garden that was overgrown with weeds, and I found her by the broken tiered fountain. She sat prim, her white lace socks pulled up to her thighs, and her knees hugged to her chest. Her taffeta dress crackled with static. The ruffles in them were stiff, gorging alleyways into her skin.

She was all greasy pigtails and vapid face. Her mouth was red around the corners. The day before, we had gone to the marketplace to get clementines for the marmalade she wanted to make. The clementine seller took her money and said, 'Thank you, pretty girl.'

And Ayosa had recoiled. She had squared her jaws and dug her hands in her pockets. All the way home, she would not talk to me – she was seething with rage. Later, she scrubbed her face raw with a pumice stone. She scrubbed her chin and cheeks and forehead, scraping off any encroaching prettiness.

When I found her in the butterfly garden, she was watching stink bugs and wax worms reel on the hot, cracked stone of the fountain. She looked up at me, and waved me closer to look at the insects too.

'It's Epitaph Day,' I said to her.

I said it with my eyes. My darling and I, we never talked to each other with our mouths.

She said, 'You want to build a bicycle?'

She showed me a dumpster in the middle of her yard, filled with scrap metal. We sifted through the pieces, ripped out the wires and fashioned them into a tandem bicycle. Then we rode the bicycle from one end of the yard to the other, our palms callused and our temples taut and our frocks withered in the moist air. Our right feet pounded the pedals and then our left feet pounded the pedals and then right-left, right-left, until our movements, and our noses, were filled with the scent of lavender, and our faces were raw from the thorns of prickly pears.

Then Mr Man found us. We did not see him until it was too late, until he was grabbing our bicycle by the handlebars, and saying, 'Wait, please!'

'Run!' I said to my darling. She made towards the apothecary's cottage to get help. Me, I did not wait for any type of help. I knew that there wasn't anyone out there who could save me from the monsters. I knew that all I had was myself. I closed my eyes and turned myself inside out, so that my soft parts were tucked away and my hard parts were outside, and then I was coursing through the air and I was hacking at Mr Man and he was wailing and wailing.

'I don't mean to hurt you,' he cried. 'Look, look, I only want to show you this!'

He reached inside his breast pocket and held out a photograph. In it was my mother, wearing her bear-fur trapper-hat, and a down parka that swept over her ankles, and she was smiling that coy smile that I knew so well. Mr Man had tears trembling in his eyes, shining like opals. He said, 'Here, take it. I will get into my car and go away now.'

This time, I was the one that ran after him, saying, 'Wait, please!'

He was tired, he said, and needed a place he could lay down his head for a while. He had driven for days to find me. I showed him the way to the shanty by the river. It was decrepit, lopsided, leaning against a parasol tree. From its porch steps, you could see the water lapping at the rocks, and the grebes and albatrosses pecking at the writhing fish, and the jacanas sunning themselves in the sand.

The shanty had belonged to GodblessAmen. He had lived inside it with his cane rats, snagging eels in the river and eating them raw, carving voodoo dolls out of wood and standing them everywhere. The voodoo dolls were still here, even though GodblessAmen and his cane rats were gone. The dolls gave me an eerie feeling, as though they were watching intensely and wielding daggers behind their backs.

'You can stay here,' I said to Mr Man. 'No one ever comes this way.'

He took his son Magnanimous off his shoulder, and slung him over a threadbare chair. He walked over to the stove and fumbled about, searching for matches, a jerrycan of kerosene, a dusty saucepan. He found lemongrass growing out back, and fetched it, and made us sweet, aromatic tea. He said, 'I met her in Moscow. Your mother, I mean. We studied at the same university. She and I, we started as comrades, and ended up as . . . Quite frankly I don't have the proper word for it. Soulmates?'

I bit my lip. 'Mr Man, are you my father?'

'Lord, no!' he said, curling his mouth as though in unimaginable horror. 'Dottie Nyairo was my sister. No, that will not do. She was not a sister at all. She was more, much, much more. A part of my soul, inhabiting a body separate from mine. Our love for each other was spiritual. It is eternal.'

I said, 'I'm awfully sorry for you. Me, all I lost was a mother. You lost a part of your soul.'

Mr Man laughed, even though I had not meant to be funny.

We sat in silence for a long while. Then Mr Man got up and lit a tea light, which was the only sort of candle he could find. 'Epitaph Day,' he said in explanation, and set the light down before us.

I stared out the window, at the jacanas. I was thinking of a dream I had recently had. In it, my mother's laughter rolled out like a great sea spreading as far as the eye could see. It was an angry sea swatting at the bustards and the finfoots and the thick-knees, sweeping them all away. Knocking dhows over and drowning those red-eyed fisher-people with dirges on their tongues. And I found a blue marlin, whose belly was inscribed with old prophecies. Saying, *Mother is made of gold and daughter is only of tarnished copper.* Saying, *Mother has a field of poppies growing on her bosom.* Saying, *Look what you did, Mbiu Dash – you spilled all her patchouli oil, now she'll never return to you.*

Mr Man squatted down at my feet, and touched my knees. 'If you don't mind, would you tell me about that day?'

'What day?'

'The day she robbed the bank.'

I did not like how close Mr Man was, so I pushed my chair back and stood up. I walked to the door and leaned against the jamb.

'Please,' Mr Man said. 'I've got to hear it.'

'I was there with her. I was in the front seat of her Volkswagen. I saw her kill two policemen with her Kalashnikov. She jumped into the car with her sack of money. We drove through the streets, and my mama tossed money notes out the window for the townspeople to take. The police were chasing us with rifles of their own. My mama tried to lose them. But they got her, in the end. She was hit twenty, thirty times. The bullet holes had her looking like a carrot grater.' I sighed, and said, 'You know the story, Mr Man. Everyone knows the story. It was all over the news.'

Mr Man stood next to me, and gazed at the paper wasps and owl flies at our feet.

'The thing I came all this way to ask is, did she *suffer*?'

I shook my head. 'I guess she did not. She laughed a lot, even when she was getting hit. She held me and laughed until all the laughter inside her was finished.'

Mr Man went and poured himself more lemongrass tea. He took a huge swig. Then he said, 'You've got to be careful. You've got to give the guilt only a knuckle, not the whole finger.'

'I've got no guilt. *She* was the one that robbed the bank. Why should I have any guilt about it?'

'Survivor's guilt.'

'You're speaking mud, Mr Man.'

'Maybe I am,' he conceded. 'In any case, I've got some. Mine follows me about like a stray mongrel.'

He was talking about his boy Magnanimous, I knew. I said, 'Tell me your story, Mr Man.'

'It's the same story as your mama's.'

'You robbed a bank?'

Mr Man shook his head. 'No, that's not what I meant,' he said. 'The lot of us, we came back from Moscow. Engineers and doctors and lawyers. All perked up and full of beans. Ready to lead our people to the promised land.'

Mr Man fell silent, lost in his thoughts. He was silent so long I thought he'd fallen asleep standing.

'Mr Man?' I said.

He blinked, and saw me, and saw where he was. He climbed down the porch steps. He said, 'Wait here a moment, I'll be back.'

He started towards the river. His son Magnanimous got up from the floor and began to follow him.

'Hey!' I said. 'Hey, Magnanimous?'

He paused by the lemongrass bushes and turned to regard me.

'What happened to *you*?' I asked.

He shrugged. 'The police came for my papa. They called out his name and then they started shooting. My papa wasn't home, thank goodness. It was just me, doing homework at the table. So I took all the bullets for my papa.'

I twisted the corner of my frock round my index finger. I said, 'What did it feel like, taking all those bullets?'

'The sky was yellow, like gooseberry. The clouds were turning, making shapes. I saw minarets, and strings of Chinese lamps, and canary birds big as airplanes. There were cowbells on my ankles and tambourines on my wrists. When I moved, there was song, and when I stopped moving there was song too. I saw pixies in cotton-candy skirts, twirling to the music of my bones. And I was laughing, and my body was falling apart, turning to millet grains, and the snipes and the wagtails were pecking at it. It felt like hallelujah.'

Mr Man returned, carrying a pair of dead, bleeding ducks. He set them down on the low table, and boiled a pot of water, and began to pluck them. He hummed as he worked, that song that went *something-something-here's-the-story-of-the-hurricane*.

'Mr Man?'

He looked up from the onion that he was dicing into quarters. 'My name's Gregory. Grey for short.'

'What happened after you returned from Moscow, all perked up and full of beans?'

He crushed a head of garlic with a hammer. He tossed the lacy garlic peels at the floor, and Magnanimous lunged at them and stuffed them into his mouth.

'They said that we got indoctrinated while we were studying in the USSR. They said that we were communists, planning a coup, supported by our Soviet sponsors. They spied on us, and stalked us, and blackmailed us, and sidelined us. Some of us got disappeared. Most of us went into hiding. Dottie, she was proud, scarlet-chested, like a parakeet. She would not come with me, no matter how much I begged. She said she was tired of playing cat and mouse. So she stayed behind to fight.'

I grimaced at his words. I could not bear to think of my mama this way, as though she had not been the type of woman who lined her eyelids with kohl and wore silk camisoles on Saturdays. Who let me have sips of her red wine as we watched *For Your Eyes Only*. Who drove out with me to the hills, so we could lie under the fever trees and eat butter cookies and read Enid Blyton books. Dottie Nyairo, who always snipped my fingernails with her front teeth. Who wore her permed hair in a beehive. Who let me stare at the sun too long, so I would get floaters in my eyes. Who made rice with fried egg for dinner most nights of the week.

Dottie Nyairo, who had been mighty proud of her name, so proud that she had taken it with her when she laughed her way out of this world. With her, I had been Mbiu Nyairo. Afterwards, the name just did not fit me right, like a cardigan that had got shrunken in the wash. Now I had a blank space where my mama's name had been. Mbiu *Dash*.

I watched as Mr Man dropped sprigs of rosemary and thyme into the bubbling pot. 'You enjoy your meal, now,' I said.

He looked up at me, his eyebrows furrowed with astonishment. 'Won't you eat?'

'I never once chewed on duck. Don't intend to start now.'

I hopped down the steps of the decayed, termite-chewed porch. Mr Man and his son Magnanimous came to the door to watch me.

'Where are you going?' Mr Man asked.

'Home.'

'Where's that?'

Look, Mr Man might have been a part of my mama's soul, but that did not mean that I was about to have him sneaking up on me in the dead of night. So, I did not tell him that I lived in the bullet-riddled Volkswagen that my mama had laughed her way out of this world in. I did not tell him that I lived with a horse called Magnolia, which I had found in the trash somewhere near Lucky Summer. I did not tell him that I lived with two hundred or so pigeons. That they were all huddled in the back seat of the Volkswagen. That I liked the way the pigeons looked – their understated elegance, the iridescence of their dress, their glossy, watchful eyes.

I shrugged, and said, 'How about you mind your own business, Mr Man?' ■

She was free from upset briefly when she heard the syncopations and the suspensions of time – the soft background music at the eatery that promised to relieve vexation. It was well blended and the rich harmony involved a bassoon.

She was there with good old Jim, in the springtime, who might have asked her, 'Do you still have intercourse? Do you bleed?'

But in real life Jim did not say anything like that and his penis was not yet sliding around her or poking.

So their moment did not become explosive and they ate their dumplings.

One of them was eager to take the paper wrapping off of the drink straw because it is the easiest thing to have trouble with, but not to fail at.

The woman sums up her son and daughter thusly when Jim inquires – Teddy is slothful and Page is satisfied to be average in every category and now she can't seem to do anything right – she is dying.

And yet the sound of the woman's indignation – its clip and its tenor – if Jim could only disregard the words – was not unappealing to his ear.

Still, Jim was fearful of what the woman might tell him next or that she might ask him a shaming question.

He was a little bit atremble further into the meal, when he sweetened up his coffee.

The woman watched him pour sugar in and stir. He poured more sugar in and stirred and next he poured in more sugar and he stirred.

As she drove herself home, the woman was hardly aware of anything except for the suggestion of roadway on account of the misty drizzle.

In these warm months – the grass and the trees and even the people – their houses and their cars and bicycles – vanished in the fog, and it was promising. And the trees were safely tucked in. Their roots were rallying in the soil, in this coil.

Would the woman also take a turn for the better in her last decade?

She felt a breeze at the top of her head while driving – and since the car windows were tightly shut, she marveled at the source of the tiny gust.

But now she had a dull ache there, in her scalp. Was that sensation *arousal*?

Well, then the rain became heavier and it made of her car's body a drum skin that produced a low-pitched, dry sound, much like applause – that is not apropos here, *not* fitting.

Because plainly there are the woman's shortcomings to consider when one compares her to other mothers – or to the huge central pool of mothers, or to the huge central pool of persons who have demonstrated that quality – *pathos*.

The woman leans forward. She can't see – can't see well enough to drive safely.

She sees only roughly splashed grays.

She did not brake the car in the middle of the road. Rather, she continued driving, while weighing the meaning of her bony hands barely holding the wheel. ■

She was so thankful for that cheerful dot in the sky!
And the sighting of the moon served Ms Bussy well as temporary encouragement. She had been weeping and she does so whenever she can – and it's sad to see how bad this is in what might be viewed as a pleasure house for some.

Gee! The full-size moon gained a victory over the woman – Dorothy Bussy (née Hiles).

But in the morning, she noted with dumbfoundment the locket that the innkeeper wore, and she thought – *Maybe, if I had bought the one like that one in Philadelphia – everything would have turned out better for me.*

People! People love lockets!

Roderica Dobson, the innkeeper, put her life story forward for Ms Bussy at breakfast and she was so happy to tell it. Also, Dobson was very beautiful, although the tale she told concerned her severe loss of reputation, as well as an appreciable sum of money.

Even so, the aura of the house produced for both women, a touch of comfort and low-key luxury. This was especially the case at the core of the house where the hall walls were covered by wallpaper bearing a pastel lily-pad theme – and there was a broad verandah with chairs.

'Are you married?' Dobson asked while Bussy plied the pastry Dobson called a *kuchen. What's a kuchen?*

'Am I married? I don't know,' Bussy said. 'Have you already eaten?'

'A plum,' Dobson said.

And in the crevices and stuck onto her lashes – sand was in lumps all in and around her eyes.

Why didn't she wash the lumps away? – or just pluck them out. Not the eyes!

Dobson was meant to represent, I believe – with her exceptional physical nature – a nearly redeeming being. To whom? To me.

Lamentably she's missed her chance. But just now I have yanked the blue frog out from a muddle at a street bazaar.

The Blue Frog. When I say those words I expect a reprieve – a tavern – tranquility.

I see myself in Ireland. We drive and I spot a road sign – TO THE BLUE FROG – and we go in and have a pint.

You have to look at the glass frog with the sun on it.

It is the sheer pool of eternity and I would like the blue frog to go down into my grave with me. ∎

In bed at night she doubles back and then turns, as if she is on a course whose curves and bends she must follow.

And she has descended into the bed wearing a gown – and the cloth twists and climbs about her.

Her daughter also has her own idea of getting somewhere. She sits in the backyard swing, while crouched down, and she kicks.

She has been dubbed Little Mary, who needs to regain strength, and she is currently her mother's burden.

But give this mother credit – she was speaking to a man while crossing the street the other day, and she was impressed with herself.

And when she spoke, she declared a purpose and such principles that we'd all be proud to honor.

And as the troop of people that the mother walked among went past several stone walls and hedges, and then past a house with a particularly complex face – the mother, of a sudden, gave up her pride in herself.

She looked dead into that face and felt that the house flaunted its royal arrogance when it refused to look directly back at her.

A laburnum in bloom and a fruit tree were equally aloof and my thought is that *all of these mothers* have to be decidedly hateful to someone, to somebody, to some persons.

So this mother of Little Mary approached a panel truck with its motor running and she was shocked by the truck's stretched-out posture.

But in time enough the truck shied away from her.

In this same district, the mother saw a house – brick below, shingles above – with all-over colors of red and gray and it displays a variety of windows – one round – one's a vertical, one horizontal.

And that house!

An important family lives in it and its overall effect is supple. It has a rounded roofline.

It is built so that its lower section is confident. Its upper zone is suspicious.

This living space shows off a nervous temperament that could persist. ■

LORENA LOHR
Untitled, 2019

CHECKOUT 19

Claire-Louise Bennett

I used tampons almost as soon as my periods began because for one thing my periods began long after everyone else had got theirs so there wasn't time to be fannying around with towels. Sanitary towels weren't cool at all by the time I began my period, tampons were the thing because they let you carry on as normal since all you had in your knickers was a little white string, which would hardly get in the way of all the activities the adverts showed menstruating girls doing, such as swirling around on roller skates, leaping into the air to catch fluorescent pink Frisbees, riding white horses across tremendous golden beaches, and so on. A lot of propaganda that was. In reality of course what carrying on as normal actually meant was, don't even think about skipping P.E. or sloping off early – don't lie down in a mute ball in the middle of the day – don't bellyache and groan at any hour of the day – don't expect to be excused from the table or let off from drying up – show up, join in, be productive – don't let the side down, never miss a day. By contrast, it was generally agreed that wearing a sanitary towel got in the way of everything. It was like having a sheep between your legs, everyone said. Only abnormal girls who had no friends in the first place and nothing to do besides didn't mind going around with a big smelly sheep wedged between their thighs all day long. Then, after years and years of wearing different sized tampons each month, and still never getting it quite right, I found myself orientating towards towels instead. It was dawning on me that I won't go on having periods forever – at some point they will splurge then weaken, become erratic, and then they will stop altogether. I should make the most of them, while they are still regular and strong, and not block them up. Blood should flow it's not a wound after all, it doesn't need to be staunched. It's peculiar, how you can do something a certain way automatically for years and years, then, when you stop and begin to do it another way, you look back on the way you did it for so long and you can't quite believe it – how you just went along with a trite and manipulative depiction of something that's in fact such an integral part of your intimate reality. Swoosh. Leap. Twirl. Shameful inculcatory nonsense. Never miss a day! I didn't even stop to consider it really, I just went along with it, hardly gave it a second thought. Until one afternoon, when I stood in the bathroom and looked at my blood and womb lining, there on a tissue, and I thought, I'll miss this when it's gone, and I realised I didn't want it congealing invisibly inside of me anymore. Towels aren't entirely plain sailing though either. I never seem to get it in quite the right place – I still manage, almost every time, to stick the bloody thing too far back along the gusset.

On the first day the colour is very pretty – it's a shade of red I've been looking for in a lipstick since forever. Neither too dark, nor too bright. Not too pink not too brown not too orange. More than once I've imagined taking the bloodstained tissue into a department store, up to the Chanel counter, the Dior counter, the Lancôme counter, and saying 'Look, this is the red, this is it, this is the most perfect red in the world. Let me see a lipstick at long last in this most perfect shade of red.' Needless to say I've never done it. Month after month I ruefully drop the most perfect shade of red down the toilet and flush it away. Quel dommage. I have this idea that Marilyn Monroe stayed in bed when she got her period and bled all over the sheets, and I'm not sure where I derived it from. It's been in my head since I was approximately ten years old. My grandmother adored old Hollywood stars, and had a particular penchant for Vivien Leigh and Marilyn Monroe, so it might have been from her I got it. But I can't imagine my grandmother telling me a thing like that. Perhaps she said it to my aunt and I overheard – I wasn't a snoop, but I did have sharp ears. My family relished exchanging grisly tales, though usually I'd only ever catch a snippet – which, severed from the full body of the story, became disturbingly visceral and took on a lasting and malignant life all of its own. I shall never forget the heinous image that assaulted my imagination when I overheard, for example, my other grandmother saying to her son, my father, 'and she'd bitten all the skin off her fingers. Imagine that, eating your own hands.' Stupidly I repeated those words to myself verbatim, many times over. My tendency to take every word I heard absolutely literally paradoxically meant I very often got the wrong end of the stick about quite a lot of things on a daily basis – and surely I had got the wrong end of the stick about this conversation – surely the girl, whoever she was, hadn't really eaten her own hands? It occurred to me that I probably hadn't understood what my grandmother had said correctly, that her words meant something else, something entirely innocuous – however instead of just brushing them off it came to me that perhaps if I only repeated the awful phrase enough, the real, innocuous meaning that it obviously contained would eventually surface in all of its forgettable ordinariness, and the gory apparition of the girl greedily gobbling up her own hands, and all the blood crawling down her arms and dripping thickly from her elbows, would go away at once. That's not what happened. On the contrary, a new terror was released upon me – ironically by the most humdrum word out of them all. After many repetitions the word 'and' lodged in my throat, expanded barbarously – I practically choked on it: *and*?! *And* she'd bitten all the skin off her fingers?? So in fact there was another thing she did, before chewing off her hands, possibly something much worse. Would my grandmother say the worst thing first? Probably she would. (My father's mother was dramatic and liked to make maximum impact when she told you a story whereas my mother's mother recounted scandalous news in a roundabout sort of way, pulled back and forth, again and again, by uncertainty and a preoccupation with peripheral details. Apparent shortcomings – oh come on, spit it out – which often nonetheless conspired to plant a strange and robust seed.) What exactly had the girl done before she chewed off the skin on her fingers? On this occasion my imagination was uncommonly considerate of my faint-hearted disposition so that instead of conjuring up the absolute worst it very quickly installed a relatively tame image of the girl tearing out her blonde and lank hair, thus preventing anything truly horrific from emerging that would scare the living daylights out of me. Tearing out her hair seemed to make sense anyway: 'She'd torn out her hair in great big clumps, and she'd bitten all the skin off her fingers. Imagine that, eating your own hands.' Yes, that made sense. Clearly it was the eating of the hands that my grandmother wanted to leave my father with, so, in all likelihood, the prior diabolical action very probably wasn't anything worse than that. And in fact, now that the hand-eating was prefixed by another grim act of self-mutilation, it wasn't nearly as frightening anymore. In fact it made me laugh.

I don't know whether Marilyn Monroe did stay in bed and bleed all over the sheets, but if she did I wouldn't blame her. Especially since she had endometriosis which meant during her period she suffered from intense pelvic pain and excruciatingly severe cramps. Sexual intercourse with male lovers would have been really uncomfortable for her a lot of the time too. My grandmother certainly wouldn't have mentioned any of that to me. She did tell me that Marilyn Monroe liked to read. 'You wouldn't think so to look at her, but she always had her head in a book. Like the way you are.' My grandmother often said 'You wouldn't think so to look at her' about some woman or another. It seemed to me that it gave her enormous pleasure, to think about women doing things and behaving in ways that were entirely at odds with what they looked like. She rarely, if ever, said such a thing about a man. She didn't talk about men very much. I got the impression she was of the opinion that, as far as men were concerned, you could tell exactly what they got up to just by looking at them. And of course you could tell what they got up to just by looking at them since they went around getting up to whatever they pleased with no compunction whatsoever – women, on the other hand, were secretive and hid things and though it may have looked like they were doing one thing they were in fact quite often doing something else entirely. By the time I was born my grandmother had already been divorced many years and would soon be living alone again since by the end of my first year in the world the younger man she'd found some overdue happiness with died of leukaemia just after Christmas. She carried on living alone until she died approximately forty years later at which point I hope that her dream of being reunited with this man she'd never stopped missing came true. It was unusual for a woman of her generation to live alone like that, for all those years, though it never seemed particularly peculiar to me growing up. We saw her often since she lived close by, and I liked going off to see her on my own, she baked fruitcake, for one thing, that tasted of marmalade and cigarettes. It was there, already cut into big squares, inside the red and cream container on the right when you went into the kitchen – or else it wasn't because she hadn't made any and that was disappointing, even if she did have something else for you. Whatever it was wouldn't taste of smoke and oranges. While I sat there eating cake, or else corned beef and beetroot with a hard-boiled egg, she'd empty her coat pockets onto the kitchen table. She was always picking things up off the street. And if you saw her in the street she'd say, 'I think I dropped something under that bench, have a look for Nanny will you.' She hadn't dropped anything of course – I was more agile than she was and could bring my eyes into places that hers couldn't investigate. 'Have a good look,' she'd say as I scrappled around beneath the bench, without ever saying what it was exactly I should be looking for. Leave no stone unturned. No. No. When I was older I worked weekends on a checkout in the local supermarket and she would often come in and watch me with abstracted admiration as I scanned frozen vegetables and tinned food. 'You look ever so smart in that uniform,' she'd say to me. Several years later I moved to another country and so I didn't see my grandmother so often anymore.

We wrote to each other now and then. In her letters she nearly always mentioned that the lady in the cigarette kiosk had asked after me. Whenever I returned and visited her we'd always have tea and fruitcake, and smoke whatever brand of menthol cigarettes she happened to prefer at the time, and then, when it was time for me to make tracks, as we always said, she'd dally up and down the hallway, offering me an assortment of things which she'd dust off with a corner of her cardigan before showing me – telephones, tea towels, slippers, irons, iced buns, umbrellas, candlesticks, air fresheners, photograph albums, gloves, 15 denier tan tights, knitting needles, manicure sets – and each time I'd explain to her regretfully that I was flying back and couldn't bring much with me. 'You're a free spirit,' she'd say. 'I don't blame you, my dear. You're better off.' Her flat was a trove of disparate objects, some mysterious, some commonplace, some utterly defunct – most of the grown-ups in my family, I noticed, seemed to think she ought to have 'a good clearout'. Yet I suspect that le Comte de Lautréamont, macabre poet and darling of the surrealists, wouldn't have endorsed their breezy incitements to declutter at all, would in fact have felt right at home in my grandmother's flat exactly as it was, since, as far as he was concerned, a sewing machine and an umbrella upon an operating table was a chance encounter of some considerable beauty. No doubt he would have found her book collection a source of considerable inspiration too. In addition to mawkish biographies of Hollywood legends my grandmother possessed an impressive range of sensational hardbacks containing photographic accounts of the vilest Victorian murders. Which is just the sort of singularity that gives an otherwise run-of-the-mill room an exciting air when you're a child. Sitting in proximity of those slashed and mangled corpses rendered in delicate monochrome made my heart thump its way into my throat in the manner of a maimed troll heaving its smeared bulk up a wishless well by the mulish efforts of its one remaining weevil-ravaged fist. I swallowed hard, again and again, until my ears thrummed, in a bid to get my heart down to where it ought to be. I'm not long for this world. I'm not long for this world.

That's something I grew accustomed to hearing my grandmother avow while waiting for instance for the kettle to boil. The dull infinite rumbling sound of water shuddering to vapour heaven knows can all of a sudden bring on such celestial yearnings. Or perhaps after, seated. While she stirred sugar into her tea and I herded cake crumbs about the tea plate on my knee with the small engrossed pad of my middle finger. She said it one day while we were both sat waiting for pudding in the living room of my aunt's house near the brook and my aunt came flying in from the kitchen holding up a large steaming spoon and said very crossly, 'Mum! Don't say things like that in front of her.' But I didn't mind, I didn't mind one bit. In fact I rather liked it when she said that and said it myself later on when I got home and was sitting on the edge of my bed. I am not long for this world. I am not long for this world. I was already experiencing the sensation by this time that I was outside of the world, looking in, and the feelings that sense mostly gave rise to were ones of forlornness and anguish. Sat on the edge of my rosebud-patterned bed, repeating my grandmother's mantra, however, I felt noble, mysterious, and independent. As if I were only visiting this world in any case and had somewhere a million times better to return to. I am not long for this world. I am not long for this world. ■

Courtesy of the author

FIRE AND ICE

Debra Gwartney

Three days before he died, my husband got out of bed. Somehow he propelled himself down the hall and into the living room, where I found him bent over a volume of Esther Horvath photographs called *Into the Arctic Ice: The Largest Polar Expedition of All Time*. Barry's white hair was sprung wild and his feet were bare though it was late at night in December, sleety rain driving against the windows. How had he pulled sweatpants over his bony hips? He'd hardly stirred all day, lifting his head only to sip on bone broth made by one of our daughters, leaning against me to get to the bathroom because he was bleary from pain drugs. Yet he'd managed to transport himself to the center of this rental house to dig out a book that now held his rapt attention.

The book had arrived by mail a few days earlier, when Barry was still able to sit on the sofa for an hour or so, and he'd turned its pages with the slightest pressure of thumb and finger so as not to mar the saturated colors of the photos. Our son-in-law was over with the rest of the family for a subdued holiday visit. The two men spoke in calm, low voices about a region of the planet once intimately familiar to my husband, second only to his knowledge of the thirty-six acres of western Oregon rainforest where he'd lived for fifty years and where I'd lived with him for nearly two decades until a wildfire booted us out one late-summer night. Barry moved closer to Pete and pointed to streaks of blue in Horvath's images of a vast icescape, the humps of polar bears, the eerie glow of human light piercing the darkness. The peeling noses and cheeks of scientists too long in the cold. I remember how he laughed with a whistle of nostalgia, missing days when he must have felt fully alive.

But now in the living room, he whipped through the pages until I heard an edge tear, a fluttering as if he'd startled a bird. When I said his name, he didn't answer. When I touched his shoulder, he jerked in my direction and insisted I start packing the car, though first he wanted me to find his suitcase and the down jacket he'd worn for forty years of polar travel. He returned to the book frantic, a man who'd dropped a key into a well's murky bottom and was crazy with the loss.

I was certain my husband was about to insist I bundle him up and drive him through the rain to our fire-damaged house, an hour away. I steeled myself for it. He'd say he had to die on his own land, near the remains of ten cords of combusted wood and his melted truck, on the smoke-saturated bed in our bedroom whose windows were still smeared orange with fire retardant. He'd check to make sure the essay he'd been working on was secure in his typewriter, waiting. Then he would rest. He'd watch through the window over the bed for flashes of kingfisher and fat rain clouds, for the sky arcs of an overwintering eagle. What nonsense it was to come to the end instead in this stranger's house with a stranger's furniture and its strange cast of light. I was sure Barry would rather use any last bursts of energy to pace the perimeter of his scorched archive, as he had most days since the fire. He'd become the lone sentry at the gates of that phantom building, which once held the history of his fifty-year writing life. For months, I'd watched him rake through the mound of ash, releasing shiny particles of the past into the smoke-stilled air. He churned up chunks of paper – cremated books that disintegrated with the slightest touch – and bent metal that he held up to the faint light in the withered forest. *What were you, then?*

Except that noise was inside my head. In fact, Barry hadn't mentioned home for over a week. What I finally put together on this Saturday night, from his various mutters and fragmented speech, was that his destination was an archipelago called Svalbard. An Arctic expedition had lost its leader, so he'd been called in to take over. He had mere hours to get there. He slammed the Horvath book shut and clambered into the spare bedroom, where he yanked out a duffel bag I'd recently emptied and stored away in my effort to make this place feel something like a home. He tossed in a broken alarm clock, a pillow, a packet of picture hangers. Where are my gloves? My Gore-Tex pants? My expedition sunglasses? Where have you put my things? Why won't you give me my things? He flailed his arms so I couldn't come close. As if the only person preventing him from the most important launch of his adventurous life was me.

And then he fell.

Barry was running – no, there was no run left in him, more an agitated hobble – back to our bedroom. He skidded on the wood floor and went flying. His hip slammed down, then his shoulder, his head bouncing against a doorframe. I cried out, and half dragged him to the bed where I wedged him under the covers. I squeezed a vial of liquid morphine into the pale ditch of his gums and sat next to him, his chest heaving, until he was asleep.

Horvath's book is about a German icebreaker called the *Polarstern*, which was allowed to become locked into sea ice off the coast of Siberia. This happened in the autumn of 2019, when the ship's engines were shut down and the vessel, lit up like an all-night casino, was left to drift, driven only by hidden ocean currents and 'at the mercy of the wind'. The ship, with more than one hundred expedition members on board at any given time, groaned through dark days and nights, destination wherever natural forces led it, mile after uncharted nautical mile into utterly undiscovered territory: 'no ship has ever ventured so far north into the central Arctic', the prologue tells us. The *Polarstern* churned through ice and storms for an entire year while an international team of scientists did what they could to record the effects of climate change.

On a thin January afternoon about a month after his death, I pulled the Horvath book from the drawer where I'd hidden it to study the photos that had so ignited my husband. I discovered in the text a mission obviously steeped in scientific logic and methodology, yet also not that far from the koans of my weekly yoga class: embrace the moment. Trust the wind to push you where you need to go. Be prepared to find your way back to center through the densest of fog. The only authentic discoveries are those that aren't forced. Stop trying to control that which is beyond your control.

Barry had been ill for a long time, but his death swooped down on us like a hawk, talons first. Startlingly fast. Everything that gave me stability and safety – our long marriage, our house, the surrounding woods, the river – was unreachable now, in dodgy shadow, and this was probably the source of my irritation toward the book in my lap. It dared to tap into what terrified me most: a reminder that there'd be no clear answers for a good long stretch; that I would have to swim in bewilderment and confusion before I could emerge on some distant shore. Solutions would roll out in front of me in their own time and at their own pace, in their own shape. In the meantime, I would have to learn to drift.

A few months earlier, on 8 September just after midnight, I found a young man on our porch holding a brick he'd been using to batter our front door. I was already awake and out of bed when I heard his pounding, his shouts to *open up*. A friend had called me minutes before, waking me from a fitful sleep. She told me to rouse my husband and get the hell out of there. I pulled on long pants, though the temperature was sweltering and the house already choked with smoke and grit. Barry was sleeping in our guest cottage that night, a few hundred feet away. I was headed there to wake him when the young man appeared on our porch hollering words my friend had already said: *Get out now*.

How odd to remember that crystallized moment, to recall how my mind slipped into the uncanny human tendency to minimize any emergency you're smack in the middle of. This could not possibly be happening to me, could it? This couldn't be how our story went. How was I to take this boy seriously with his lace-up boots and flannel shirt, red suspenders holding up canvas pants? I let myself imagine someone was just around the corner filming this non-crisis, this rumor of terror and destruction. Otherwise, what was with the klieg lights over-illuminating the woods around our home with a pumpkin-tinted hue as if we'd all been transported into a Wes Anderson movie?

You need to go now, the young firefighter said. *You need to hurry.*

B arry and I had argued some hours before the phone call from our friend, before the brick-wielding man on the porch, a spat between us that gnaws at me still. I think of it, our last argument on our last night in our own home, as one of those bullhorn warnings that sound at certain points in a marriage. As in: it's time to take account of where you're at, as individuals and as a couple. Seven years post cancer diagnosis, my husband's stamina and drive were still remarkable, the mainstay of his character, and yet there was no missing the increasing pain in his spine and ribs, his body's insistence on deep, long naps, his papery skin now drained of color. He had fewer hours of focus and attention and he meant to give those to an essay he'd begun, and after that to other pieces he'd sketched out to prove (mostly to himself) that in the wake of the latest book, published a year earlier to vibrant acclaim, he would continue on with his legendary verve and purpose. Barry was quite fixed on the idea that a writer is writing *today*, not dozing in the soft nest of what he (in this case) wrote yesterday. As for me, I had published a book in the same month as Barry's *Horizon*, though mine pretty much landed with a thud and garnered little notice. I'd composed hardly a paragraph since, and was plunged into doubt, plagued with a truth I didn't want to face about my late-in-life prospects. I begged Barry to escape with me, to run away. We'd fly to Barcelona, Costa Rica, the two of us alone in a new land where I didn't have to stare at my desk with its yank of defeat. But even as he was unfurling a map of Spain, spreading it wide on our table, running a light pencil line from Madrid to Lisbon across the border, I knew we wouldn't go.

Here was an ongoing tension in our marriage: I often wanted us to slip off together, just us. No obligations, no university speeches or community gatherings, no award ceremonies. But Barry found it nearly impossible to disrupt the rhythm of his writing life for reasons of rest and relaxation, and rarely did so. This often led to stiffness between us, harsh words. But this time I surprised myself. As he rolled up the map while saying something about how we'd go *as soon as I finish* . . . I waited for the disappointment that usually thrummed in me when plans were put off. But it wasn't there. I saw that he was past traveling now, no matter what part of the world called to him as a writer, and no matter how adamant I was about days together away from the hubbub. Now he needed to be home. Home is what fed him. He fit hand in glove at his small desk overlooking the river, tight in his narrow chair, fingers on his typewriter keys, his pile of research books at the ready and pencils sharpened to fine, dustless points.

The evening of our argument I was grilling our dinner. I had returned two days earlier from Idaho, where I'd sat with my mother in her final hours and stayed for a week to arrange, with my siblings, a small family burial service under the beating sun, since Covid-19 dictated we stay strictly outdoors. At home on this evening, it was too early for dusk, but smoke from a nearby wildfire dimmed and dulled the summer light. Barry stood at the far end of our deck, double-masked, refusing to step closer to me in case I'd been infected by the niece I'd hugged, the daughter who drove with me, a gas station attendant, the man who took my mother's burial clothes from me at the mortuary. Barry and I had both agreed that it was too risky for him to go to Idaho, but now that I was back, I was aching to be held, aching to spool out my version of the disorientation one feels after losing a parent. I wanted my husband to ignore the coronavirus rules, this once, but he wasn't ready to take the chance.

He proposed that we instead talk out on the deck with six feet between us. I hated the idea and fumed at him for bringing it up. For one thing, we had to raise our voices over the roar of an unusual wind, an unbidden wind, that whipped the 150-foot trees around us as if they were blades of grass. Dense smoke pillowed in the sky, and, when my phone beeped, I read Barry a text from various authorities instructing us not to panic, but to stay indoors – indoors! – with windows closed and to stop calling 911. The smoke was from a distant conflagration, that message explained. *A fire that poses no danger to you.*

Later, I'd bring it up with neighbors – those of us who'd escaped our burning river valley that September night – this curse of technology, the way we'd all been tripped by miscommunications and the confusion that reigned about what to do and when to do it. But that was still to come. For now, without a notion of what was racing toward us, our standoff on the deck continued, neither Barry nor I willing to give in to the other. *Come here, go away.* Months after he'd died, in anguish over that final night at our house, I would try to parse our code, our meaning. What it was we were trying to say to each other. Some version of: *I don't want to go on without you. You must figure out how to go on without me.* Neither of us admitting that we were running out of time.

I dished up fish and vegetables, my spoon cracking against his plate and then against mine. He picked up his food, his fork and his knife. He said, 'Please. Give me a few days,' and I watched him walk to our guest cottage and snap the door closed.

When I jumped down the back stairs, rushing to the cottage to wake Barry, I was smacked by the light I'd noticed a minute earlier behind the boy on the porch. I turned around into the sucking exhale of a hillside fully on fire, hoodoo flames leaping from the ridges, an orange glow washing over trees and sky. Over me. The crackle, the roar of it. The snowy ash. I shouted my husband's name, I pounded on the locked door. He opened up, startled and wide-eyed. 'We have to go,' I said.

Within five minutes, we did go, with two firefighters now ushering us into the car. I threw our hissing cat – Barry had dragged her from under the bed – onto the back seat. I had my purse slung over a shoulder, but that was it. He had nothing but the clothes he was wearing, not his wallet, not his cancer drugs, not the manuscript he'd been writing over the days I was away. But of course there was no going back, even after we thought of things we were desperate for. Or even when, a half-mile from our house, we were stopped by a cedar tree toppled in the road, flames sparking from its branches. Two men in the car in front of us hopped out – one already revving a chainsaw. They also knew our only choice was to push on. Barry unclicked his seat belt and made moves to join them. I grabbed his arm. 'Don't,' I said to the man who for fifty years was the first to arrive at every such dilemma, ready to act, to solve. 'This once, please don't.'

For me, he stayed.

We drove ahead in a procession of maybe 200 cars. The cat in the back seat yowled without ceasing so we didn't have to. Within a few miles we were beyond the fire – but it would catch up, soon. It would burn for weeks. It would consume 173,000 acres and 500 structures. None of us would be allowed back in for over a week, and only then with a police escort, to stand on our respective properties and witness for ourselves the transformative power of fire. Barry and I stepped out of a sheriff's car that day to find our house intact – one of the few on the river that firefighters managed to save. It looked as if it had been picked up by a claw and flung onto a pile of rubble. It looked broken and stunned. Still, we wept with relief.

We'd done little but sit in a hotel room those first few days after evacuation, answering a barrage of phone calls and emails. It was one of those pet hotels – we were consigned to such a place because of our cat, though it was dogs that barked in the hallways and left puddles of pee on the lobby floor and caused our kitty to press into the far reaches of a closet, where we'd sprinkle her favorite treats and set a bowl of fresh water. Over and over we were warned not to go outdoors. The air in this town now registered as the most toxic in the world, worse than any industrialized city in China or India, worse than the notorious bad air of Mexico City. On the day I write this, the worst air quality index in the world was measured in Dhaka, Bangladesh: 313. In those first days in the hotel, the AQI was over

500, and one morning it reached 800. We were breathing our cars, our refrigerators, our metal roofs and generators. Dead birds and bobcat and bear and elk. And of course, we were breathing our trees.

Did we have a home? We didn't know then, couldn't know, for the first ten-day stretch, and this is what Barry explained to his oncologist, a woman he trusted and loved, when she appeared on the screen of my laptop for a Zoom appointment. She had come to deliver her own bitter news: the drugs that had for years kept Barry's cancer from growing, that prevented new metastatic lesions beyond those cemented in his pelvic region and ribs, were no longer working. The cancer had found new purchase in his bones and in his blood. Beyond clinical trials and palliative medications, she had no treatment to offer.

We hung up with her. I put the computer away and went down to the hotel restaurant to order the same mediocre sandwiches we'd eaten the day before. We watched the election news. Barry sprinkled cat treats in the closet. I stuffed towels around the windows. We read our books, got into our bed. We drifted.

It took me several months to locate a rental house that we both felt was right. On three acres, sun-drenched, clean and welcoming. We could settle here and make decisions – that's what we both believed; this was the mini-relief we gave in to. But on the third morning here, while I was cooking oatmeal, I heard a crash in the spare bedroom. When I rounded the corner, I saw Barry on the floor, tangled in the drawers of a bureau that had fallen with him. The side of his head was gushing blood. I followed the ambulance I'd called to the hospital, but was told at the door that coronavirus protocol prevented me from entering the emergency room. 'Go home,' a nurse told me. 'We'll phone you as soon as we know something.'

I was nearly at the rental house when my phone rang. It was the ER doctor. He told me that Barry's heart had failed, a total block, and that he'd been shocked five times with the defibrillator to bring him back. 'If he codes again,' this doctor asked me, 'do you want us to resuscitate him?'

I instantly convinced myself that the doctor had reached the wrong person, dialed the wrong number. My husband had taken a fall and likely had suffered a concussion, that was all. Right? This other thing about hearts and shocks couldn't be happening to us. Hadn't we endured enough? But then a few days later the hospital released Barry into my care. It was clear he had nearly reached the end. I drove him back to the house where we met with a hospice nurse. She'd brought a box of drugs. This one for pain, this one for worse pain, this for hallucinations, this for panic. *We'll use none of them*, I told myself, *she doesn't know how strong he is* (we used them all). The nurse also told us Barry would likely not survive a trip to our home on the river. The rental house is where he would die.

The morning after Barry's near escape to Svalbard, I woke early. I'd been up every few hours to give him his pain drugs, to check his breathing, to wash the crust from his lips. I rose in the fluid winter light to slip into the kitchen so I could call our same nurse. I'd tell her that something had changed, a shift in him, a shift in me, and it was time, as she'd told me it soon would be, to bring in a hospital bed to set up in the living room. That way we could all – the four daughters and I – take turns keeping him company, making him comfortable. I'd resisted the finality of the hospital bed, as some part of me believed my husband would rally one last time. He was famous for it. Crisis after crisis with his health over the past year, until doctors were sure he was done for. But my husband would gather up that Barry Lopez resolve and determination and mighty bone strength, and he'd stand on his feet. I almost expected it again today: Barry sauntering around the corner in the same flannel shirt and sweatpants he'd worn the day before, thick wool socks on his feet, asking about a cup of coffee, asking about the *New York Times* headlines while the cat rubbed against his legs in her bid for breakfast.

But I was alone and I leaned against the counter in this strange house and took in the first of the lasts. The last night we would sleep in a bed together, the last time we'd choose a movie to watch, the last meal I'd make for him, the last music he'd put on to well through the living room. I'd overheard a conversation between Barry and his young friend John the day before about that last essay still rolled in the typewriter at home – there was an exuberance in my husband's voice I hadn't heard for a long while. The talk between the two men had sprung open a clarity of mind Barry was known for, the next revision cooking on high in him now. When they hung up, Barry wrote down three simple lines, or maybe a series of words. I don't remember, though I do recall a pinch of envy in my own rib cage. His rush of happiness, this lifting of a burden, was in reference to the final piece Barry intended to write and not the chance to spend diminishing hours with me. We hadn't said much about the inevitable parting from each other; I was waiting for him to begin the conversation, whatever words we still had to say. He finished his note and asked me to put the scrap of paper on the desk, which I did. Weeks down the road, I'd think of it, but in the hubbub of moving furniture and candles and loved ones in and out of the room, the paper had been lost. The shape of an essay that died with its author.

I went back to the bedroom now and saw that Barry was beginning to stir. I pulled away the covers and got into bed with this man I'd loved for twenty-some years, who helped me raise daughters, and who was cracked open by grandchildren in a way he couldn't imagine he was capable of. I could feel his heat, hear his breath, but I made myself accept that he might already be gone, that I had let him leave without a proper farewell, without speaking in the language of our long intimacy. Maybe Barry was on the ice now, leading his ideal expedition. With sled dogs straining at the bit, fat mittens on his hands and goggles protecting his eyes, his exhalations frosting the air around his mouth. He was journeying across the wide sweep of the Arctic and, like the scientists aboard the *Polarstern*, eager to take in whatever the land and sea deigned to offer him. Barry was not one to invest in answers. It was the questions that pulsed in his body and propelled him forward no matter where he traveled in the world.

But me – I had questions and I did want answers. How was I to make peace with my husband's disappearance before he had actually disappeared? How was I to give up on a last chance to express what we meant to each other? I rolled toward him, careful to stay clear of ribs that exploded in pain with the slightest brush. He opened his eyes. He turned to look at me.

'Barry, do you know who I am?' I said.

He reached over to put his palm on my face. He said my name. He said, 'Debra,' and an ease filled me like honey. In the middle of lonely nights now, I try to remember the warmth of it in my arms and legs, the way it opened up in my belly. He wouldn't say my name again; I wasn't sure he would recognize me again. It was the last time we'd be alone. I would learn to live with that, because I had this memory now. For a beat of a few seconds there was no one but us, the two of us undisturbed in our marriage bed, floating on our distant sea. ■

CONTRIBUTORS

Kaveh Akbar's poems have appeared in the *New Yorker*, the *Paris Review*, the *New York Times*, *Best American Poetry* and elsewhere. He is the author of two books of poetry – *Pilgrim Bell* and *Calling a Wolf a Wolf* – and the editor of *The Penguin Book of Spiritual Verse: 100 Poets on the Divine*. Born in Tehran, Iran, Akbar teaches at Purdue University and in the low-residency MFA programmes at Randolph and Warren Wilson colleges. Currently, he serves as Poetry Editor for the *Nation*.

Jesse Ball (b. 1978, New York) is known for absurd and philosophical works of social criticism, often in the form of novels. His prize-winning books have been published in many languages. Since 2007 he has been on the faculty of the School of the Art Institute of Chicago.

Claire-Louise Bennett is the author of *Pond* and *Fish Out of Water*. 'Checkout 19' is taken from her novel of the same title, forthcoming from Jonathan Cape in 2021.

Sasha Debevec-McKenney is the 2020–21 Jay C. and Ruth Halls Poetry Fellow at the University of Wisconsin Institute for Creative Writing, and she received her MFA from New York University. She was born in Hartford, Connecticut.

Chris Dennis is a writer and public health educator from southern Illinois. He is the author of *Here Is What You Do*. Other work has appeared in *Granta*, the *Paris Review*, *Playgirl*, *McSweeney's*, *Literary Hub* and *Guernica*. He holds a master's degree from Washington University in St Louis, where he also received a postgraduate fellowship.

Eva Freeman's short fiction has appeared in *Catamaran*, *Salt Hill* and *Black Renaissance/Renaissance Noire*, among others. She teaches writing at Baruch College and recently completed her first novel. She lives in Brooklyn with her family.

Sara Freeman is a Canadian British writer based in the US. She graduated from Columbia University with an MFA in fiction in 2013, where she was awarded the Henfield Prize for the best piece of short fiction by a graduate student. 'Tides' is an extract from her debut novel of the same name, forthcoming in 2022 from Granta Books in the UK, Grove Atlantic in the US and Hamish Hamilton in Canada.

Debra Gwartney is the author of two memoirs, *Live Through This* and *I Am a Stranger Here Myself*. Her essay 'Suffer Me to Pass' was selected for a Pushcart Prize. She lives in western Oregon.

Colin Herd is a poet and lecturer at the University of Glasgow. His collections include *Too Ok, Glovebox, Click + Collect* and *You Name It.*

Ruchir Joshi is a writer and film-maker. His novel, *The Last Jet-Engine Laugh*, was published in 2000. His forthcoming novel, *Great Eastern Hotel*, will be published by HarperCollins in the UK and India.

Robbie Lawrence is a Scottish photographer based in London. Working primarily in long-form documentary, he has photographed projects in the Congo, Faroe Islands, Sierra Leone and in the US city of Savannah, Georgia. In 2019 his first monograph, *Blackwater River*, was published by Stanley/Barker. The book was featured on the cover of the *British Journal of Photography* and named the *New Statesman*'s photo book of the year.

Tao Lin is the author of ten books of prose and poetry, including the novels *Leave Society* and *Taipei* and the memoir *Trip*. He edits Muumuu House and lives in Hawaii.

Kaitlin Maxwell is a photographer born in Florida in the early 90s. She received her BFA from the School of Visual Arts and her MFA from Yale School of Art, where she was awarded the Richard Benson Prize for excellence in photography. Her photographs have appeared in the *New Yorker*, the *New York*

Times, Vogue Spain and *Clan Photo Magazine.*

Sandra Newman is the author of four novels, including *The Heavens* and *The Country of Ice Cream Star*. Her fifth novel, *The Men*, will be published by Granta Books in 2022. She's also the author of four works of non-fiction, including *How Not to Write a Novel* (with Howard Mittelmark).

Gboyega Odubanjo was born and raised in east London. He is the author of two poetry pamphlets: *While I Yet Live* and *Aunty Uncle Poems*. Odubanjo is one of the editors of the poetry magazine *bath magg.*

Okwiri Oduor was born in Nairobi, Kenya. In 2014, she won the Caine Prize for African Writing for her story 'My Father's Head'. A graduate of the Iowa Writers' Workshop, her first novel, *Things They Lost*, will be published in 2022.

Adam O'Fallon Price is the author of two novels, *The Grand Tour* and *The Hotel Neversink*, winner of the 2020 Edgar Award for Best Paperback Original. His short fiction has appeared in *Harper's Magazine*, the *Paris Review, Granta, VICE* and many other places, and his essays and criticism regularly appear in the *Paris Review* Daily, *Ploughshares, Electric Literature,* and *The Millions*, where he's a staff writer.

Vanessa Onwuemezi is a writer and poet living in London. Her work has appeared in *Prototype*, *frieze* and *Five Dials*. Her story 'At the Heart of Things' won the *White Review* Short Story Prize in 2019.

Kathryn Scanlan is the author of *Aug 9—Fog* and *The Dominant Animal*. She lives in Los Angeles and is the recipient of a 2021 Literature Award from the American Academy of Arts and Letters.

Lynne Tillman writes novels, stories and essays. Her most recent novel is *Men and Apparitions*; in October 2021, her novella *Weird Fucks* is forthcoming with Peninsula Press. In 2022, her book-length autobiographical essay, *Mothercare*, will be published by Soft Skull Press. Tillman has written on many artists and writers, including Andy Warhol, Paula Fox, Laurie Simmons, Susan Hiller, Jane Bowles, Steve Locke, Harry Mathews, Rosalind Fox Solomon and Stephen Shore. She has received a Guggenheim Fellowship and a Creative Capital/Warhol Foundation grant for arts writing.

Diane Williams is the author of nine books of fiction, including *The Collected Stories of Diane Williams*. A new book of her stories, *How High? – That High*, is forthcoming from Soho Press in 2021. She is also the founder and editor of the literary annual *NOON*. She lives in New York City.